Children of l

Anzia Yezierska

Alpha Editions

This edition published in 2024

ISBN : 9789367241066

Design and Setting By
Alpha Editions
www.alphaedis.com
Email - info@alphaedis.com

Contents

MOSTLY ABOUT MYSELF

I feel like a starved man who is so bewildered by the first sight of food that he wants to grab and devour the ice-cream, the roast and the entrée all in one gulp. For ages and ages, my people in Russia had no more voice than the broomstick in the corner. The poor had no more chance to say what they thought or felt than the dirt under the feet.

And here, in America, a miracle has happened to me. I can lift up my head like a person. After centuries of suppression I am allowed to speak. Is it a wonder that I am too excited to know where to begin?

All the starved, unlived years crowd into my throat and choke me. I don't know whether it is joy or sorrow that hurts me so. I only feel my release is wrung with the pain of all those back of me who lived and died, their dumbness pressing down on them like stories on the heart.

My mother, who dried out her days fighting at the pushcarts for another potato, another onion into the bag, wearing out her heart and soul and brain with the one unceasing worry—how to get food for the children a penny cheaper—and my father, a Hebrew scholar and dreamer who was always too much up in the air to come down to such sordid thoughts as bread and rent, and the lost and wasted lives of my brothers and sisters and my grandfather and grandmother, and all those dumb generations back of me, are crying in every breath of every word that is struggling itself out of me.

I am the mad mob at a mass meeting, shouting, waving with their hands and stamping with their feet, to their leader: "Speech! Speech!" And I am also the bewildered leader struggling to say something and make myself heard through the deafening noise of a thousand clamouring voices.

I envy the writers who can sit down at their desks in the clear, calm security of their vision and begin their story at the beginning and work it up logically, step by step, till they get to the end.

With me, the end and the middle and the beginning of my story whirl before me in a mad blur. And I cannot sit still inside myself till the vision becomes clear and whole and sane in my brain. I'm too much on fire to wait till I understand what I see and feel. My hands rush out to seize a word from the end, a phrase from the middle, or a sentence from the beginning. I jot down any fragment of a thought that I can get hold of. And then I gather these fragments, words, phrases, sentences, and I paste them together with my own blood.

Think of the toil it takes to wade through a dozen pages that you must cut down into one paragraph. Sometimes the vivisection I must commit on myself to create one little living sentence leaves me spent for days.

I thought when the editor asked me to write mostly about myself, telling of my own life, it would be so simple the thing would write itself. And just look at me at my desk! Before me are reams of jumbled pages of madness and inspiration, and I am trying to make a little sense of it all.

What shall I keep, and what shall I throw away? Which is madness, and which is inspiration? I never know. I pick and choose things like a person feeling his way in the dark. I never know whether the thoughts I've discarded are not perhaps better than the thoughts I've kept. With all the physical anguish I put into my work, I am never sure of myself. But I am sure of this, that the utterance of the ignorant like me is something like the utterance of the dying. It's mixed up and incoherent, but it has in it the last breath of life and death.

I am learning to accept the torture of chaos and confusion and doubt through which my thoughts must pass, as a man learns to accept a hump on his back, or the loss of an arm, or any affliction which the fates thrust upon him.

I am learning, as I grow older, to be tolerant with my own inadequacy. I am learning slowly to stop wasting myself trying to make myself over on the pattern of some better organized, more educated person than I am. I no longer waste precious time wishing for the brains of a George Eliot, or the fluency of a George Sand, or the marvellous gift of words of a May Sinclair. Here I am as I am, and life is short and work is long. With this limited brain of my inadequate self I must get the most work done. I can only do the best I can and leave the outcome in the hands of the Higher Powers.

I am aware that there's a little too much of I—I—I, too much of self-analysis and introspection in my writing. But this is because I was forced to live alone with myself so much. I spent most of my youth at work I hated, work which called only for the use of the hands, the strength of my body—not my heart, not my brain. So my thoughts, instead of going out naturally to the world around me, were turned in upon myself.

I look upon my self-analysis and introspection as so much dirt through which I have to dig before I can come into the light of objectivity and see the people of the worlds around me.

Writing is to me a confession—not a profession. I know a man, a literary hack who calls himself a dealer in words. He can write to order on any subject he is hired to write about. I often marvel at the swift ease with which he can turn from literary criticism to politics, or psycho-analysis. A fatal fluency enables him to turn out thousands of words a day in the busy factory of his brain, without putting anything of himself into it.

But I can never touch the surfaces of things. I can only write from the depths. I feel myself always under the aching weight of my thoughts. And words are luring lights that beckon to me through the thick mist of vague, dumb thoughts that hang over me and press down on me.

I am so in love with the changing lights and shades of words that I almost hate their power over me, as you hate the tyranny of the people you love too much. I almost hate writing, because I love so passionately to express the innermost and outermost of my thoughts and feelings. And the words I write are never what I started out to express, but what came out of my desire for expression.

Often I read my own writing as though it were somebody else's. My own words mock at me with their glaring unreality. Where is that burning vividness of things that possessed me when I began? Why did I kill myself so for nothing? Are these stiff, stilted words me?

I stare at the pages that represent so many days and nights of labour more bitter, more violent, than childbirth. What has happened? Has my terrific passion for giving out my experiences only built a barrier of barren words against the experience that I held so close?

It's as if every kiss, every embrace of the lover and the beloved instead of fusing them into a closer oneness only drew them farther and farther apart. Every written word instead of bringing the vision nearer only pushed it farther and farther away.

But the sense of failure never stops me. It only spurs my sleeping senses with ever new inexhaustible energy to do the one thing over and over and over again till I touch nearer the edge of that flaming reality just beyond reach.

Writing is ordinarily the least part of a man. It is all there is of me. I want to write with every pulse of my blood and every breath of my spirit. I want to write waking or dreaming, year in and year out. I burn up in this all-consuming desire my family, my friends, my loves, my clothes, my food, my very life.

And yet the minute my writing gets into print I hate the sight of it. I have all the patience in the world to do over a page a thousand times. But the moment it gets out of my hand I can't bear to touch it with a pitchfork. The minute a manuscript gets into print it's all dead shells of the past to me.

I know some people who hate the books I write, and because they hate my books they hate me. I want to say to them now that I, too, hate the stuff I write. Can't we be friends and make the mutual hatred of my books a bond instead of a barrier? My books are not me.

Is this a contradiction of anything I said in the page above? I do not claim to be logical or consistent. I do not claim to think things out; I only feel out my feelings, and the only thing true about feelings is that they change and become different in the very process of utterance. The minute I say a thing with the absolute sincerity of my being, up rushes another thought that hits my most earnest sincerity in the face and shows it up for a lie.

I am alive, and the only thing real in my aliveness is the vitality of unceasing change. Sometimes I wake up in the morning with a fresh new thought that sweeps out of the window all of the most precious thoughts of the day before.

Perhaps by the time I shall have reached the end of this little sketch I shall have refuted every statement I tried to make at the beginning. I cannot help it. I am not attempting to write a story to fit into the set mould of a magazine. I am trying to give you the changing, baffling, contradictory substance of which my life is made.

I remember my mother's ecstatic face when she burst into the house and announced proudly that, though she never had had a chance to learn the alphabet, she could read the names of the streets and she could find her way to the free dispensary without having to be led by us.

"I'm no longer blind," she cried, tossing up her market basket in a gesture of triumph. "The signs of the streets are like pictures before my eyes. Delancey Street has the black hooks one way, and Essex Street has black hooks the other way." She tore off her blue-checked apron. "I can also be a lady and walk without having to beg people to show me the way."

Something of my mother's wonder was mine when, without knowing the first alphabet of literature, I had discovered that Beauty was anywhere a person tries to think out his thoughts. Beauty was no less in the dark basement of a sweat-shop than in the sunny, spacious halls of a palace. So that I, buried alive in the killing blackness of poverty, could wrest the beauty of reality out of my experiences no less than the princess who had the chance to live and love and whose only worry was which of her adorers should she choose for a husband.

I did not at first think it as clearly as I write it now. In fact, I did not think then at all. I only felt. And it gave me a certain power over the things that weighed over me, merely saying out on paper what I felt about them.

My first alphabet of self-expression was hatred, wrath and rebellion. Once during lunch-hour while the other girls in the shop were eating and talking and laughing, I wrote out on my greasy lunch-bag the thoughts that were boiling in me for a long, long time.

"I hate beautiful things," I began. "All day long I handle beautiful clothes, but not for me—only for others to wear. The bloated rich with nothing but cold cash can buy the beautiful things made with the sweat of my hands, while I choke in ugliness." Merely writing out the wildness running through my head enabled me to wear the rags I had to wear with a certain bitter defiance.

But after a while, raving at things in the air ceased to bring me relief. I felt a little like my mother yelling and cursing at the children and the worries around her without knowing what or where. I felt like a woman standing in the middle of her upset house in the morning—beds not made, dishes not washed, dirty clothes and rags hanging over the chairs, all the drawers pushed out in mixed-up disorder, the broom with the dirt in the middle of the floor—and she not knowing where to begin.

I wanted order, order in my head. But then I was too mixed up with too many thoughts to put anything in its place. In a blind sort of way, in groping for order I was groping for beauty. I felt no peace in what I wrote unless I could make my words laugh and cry with the life of the poor I was living. I was always digging, digging for the beauty that I sensed back of the dirt and the disorder. Until I could find a way to express the beauty of that reality there was no rest in me. Like the woman who makes the beds or sweeps the house and lets the rest go, so I took hold of one idea at a time and pushed all the other ideas out of my head. And day and night I burned up my body and brain with that one idea till it got light all around me—the light of an idea that shaped itself in a living picture of living people.

When I saw my first story in print I felt bigger than Columbus who discovered the New World. I felt bigger than the man who built Brooklyn Bridge or the highest skyscraper in New York. I walked the streets, holding the magazine tight in my hands, laughing and crying to myself: "I had an idea and I thought it out. I did it, I did it! I'm not a crazy fool, I'm not a crazy fool!"

But the next day all my fiery gladness turned cold. I saw how far from the whole round circle of the idea was my printed story. And I was burning to do the same thing over again from another side, to show it up more.

Critics have said that I have but one story to tell, and that I tell that one story in different ways each time I write. That is true. My one story is hunger. Hunger driven by loneliness.

But is not all of human life but the story of our hunger, our loneliness? What is at the root of economics, sociology, literature and all art but man's bread hunger and man's love hunger?

When I first started to write I could only write one thing—different phases of the one thing only—bread hunger. At last I've written out my bread hunger. And now I can write only the different phases of the one thing only—loneliness, love hunger, the hunger for people.

In the days of poverty I used to think there was no experience that tears through the bottom of the earth like the hunger for bread. But now I know, more terrible than the hunger for bread is the hunger for people.

I used to be more hungry after a meal than before. Years ago, the food I could afford to buy only whetted my appetite for more food. Sometimes after I had paid down my last precious pennies for a meal in one of those white-tiled restaurants, I'd get so mad with hunger I'd want to dash the empty dishes at the heads of the waiters and cry out like a lunatic: "Don't feed me with plates and forks and tablecloths. I want real food. I want to bite into huge chunks of meat. I want butter and quarts of milk and eggs—dozens of eggs. I want to fill up for once in my life."

This unacted madness used to be always flying through my brain, morning, noon and night. Whenever I wanted to think, my thoughts were swept away by the sight of thick, juicy steaks and mounds of butter and platters full of eggs.

Now I no longer live in a lonely hall-room in a tenement. I have won many friends. I am invited out to teas and dinners and social affairs. And I wonder, is my insatiable hunger for people so great because for so many centuries my race has been isolated in Ghettos, shut out of contact with others? Here in America for the first time races, classes and creeds are free to meet and mingle on planes as high and wide as all humanity and its problems. And I am aching to touch all the different races, classes and creeds at all possible points of contact, and I never seem to have enough of people.

When I first came to America the coldness of the Americans used to rouse in me the fury of a savage. Their impersonal, non-committal air was like a personal insult to me. I longed to shake them out of their aloofness, their frozen stolidity. But now when I meet an Anglo-Saxon I want to cry out to him: "We're friends, we're friends, I tell you! We understand the same things, even though we seem to be so different on the outside."

Sometimes a man and a woman are so different that they hate each other at first sight. Their intense difference stabs a sharp sword of fear into each heart. But when this fear that froze each into his separate oppositeness ever has a chance for a little sun of understanding, then the very difference that drew them apart pulls them closer than those born alike. Perhaps that accounts for the devouring affinity between my race and the Anglo-Saxon race.

In my early childhood my people hammered into me defeat, defeat, because that was the way they accepted the crushing weight of life. Life had crushed my mother, so without knowing it she fed defeat with the milk of her bosom into the blood and bone of her children. But this thing that stunted the courage, the initiative, of the other children roused the fighting devils in me.

When yet barely able to speak, I began to think and question the justice of the world around me and to assert my rights.

"Mamma," I asked out of a clear sky, "why does Masha Stein have butter on her bread every morning, and why is our bread always hard and dry, and nothing on it?"

"Butter wills itself in you!" shrieked my mother, as she thrust the hash of potato peelings in front of me for my noonday meal. "Have you got a father a business man, a butcher or a grocer, a breadgiver, like Masha Stein's father? You don't own the dirt under Masha's doorstep. You got a father a scholar. He holds himself all day with God; he might as well hang the beggar's bag on his neck and be done with it."

At the time I had no answer. I was too young to voice my revolt against my mother's dark reasoning. But the fact that I did not forget this speech of so many years ago shows how her black pessimism cut against my grain.

I have a much clearer memory of my next rebellion against the thick gloom in which my young years were sunk.

"Mamma, what's a birthday?" I cried, bursting into the house in a whirl of excitement. "Becky, the pawnbroker's girl on the block, will have a birthday to-morrow. And she'll get presents for nothing, a cake with candles on it, and a whole lot of grand things from girls for nothing—and she said I must come. Could I have a birthday, too, like she?"

"Woe is to me!" cried my mother, glaring at me with wet, swollen eyes. "A birthday lays in your head? Enjoyments lays in your head?" she continued bitterly. "You want to be glad that you were born into the world? A whole lot you got to be glad about. Wouldn't it be better if you was never born already?"

At the harsh sound of my mother's voice all my dreams took wing. In rebellion and disappointment I thrust out my lips with a trembling between retort and tears. It was as if the devil himself urged my mother thus to avenge herself upon her helpless children for the aches and weariness of her own life. So she went on, like a horse bolting downhill, feeling the pressure of the load behind him.

"What is with you the great joy? That you ain't got a shirt on your back? That you ain't got no shoes on your feet? Why are you with yourself so happy? Is it because the landlord sent the moving bill, and you'll be laying in the street to-morrow, already?"

I had forgotten that we had received a notice of eviction, for unpaid rent, a few days before. A frenzy of fear had taken possession of my mother as she anticipated the horror of being thrown into the street. For hours at a time I would see her staring at the wall with the glassy stare of a madwoman.

"With what have you to be happy, I ask only?" she went on. "Have you got money laying in the bank? Let the rich people enjoy themselves. For them is the world like made to order. For them the music plays. They can have birthdays. But what's the world to the poor man? Only one terrible, never-stopping fight with the groceryman and the butcher and the landlord."

I gazed at my mother with old, solemn eyes, feeling helplessly sucked into her bitterness and gloom.

"What's a poor man but a living dead one?" she pursued, talking more to herself than to me. "You ought to light a black candle on your birthday. You ought to lie on your face and cry and curse the day you was born!"

Crushed by her tirade, I went out silently. The fairy dream of the approaching birthday had been rudely shattered. Blinded with tears, I sat down on the edge of the gutter in front of our tenement.

"Look, these are the pink candles for the birthday cake!" A poke in the back from Becky startled me. "Aren't they grand? And mamma will buy me a French doll, and papa said he'd give me a desk, and my aunt will give me a painting set, and every girl that comes will bring me something different."

"But what's the use?" I sobbed. "I ain't got nothing for no present, and I can't come—and my mother is so mean she got mad and hollered like hell because I only asked her about the birthday, and——"

A passionate fit of sobbing drowned my words.

In an instant Becky had her arms about me. "I want you to come without a present," she said. "I will have a lot of presents, anyhow."

Assured of her welcome I went the next day. But as I opened the door fear seized me. I paused trembling, holding the knob in my hand, too dazed by the sight before me to make a step. More than the strangeness of the faces awed me. Ordinary home comforts, cushioned chairs, green ferns between white curtains, the bright rugs on the floor were new and wonderful to me. Timorously I edged my way into the room, so blinded by the shimmering colours of the cakes and fruits and candies that covered the table that I did not see Becky approaching me with outstretched arms.

"Mamma, this is that little immigrant girl who never had a birthday," she said, "so I wanted to show her mine."

Becky's father glanced at her all in white, with pink ribbons on her curls, as she stood beside me in my torn rags reeking with the grime of neglect. A shudder of revulsion went through him at the sight of me.

"See what Becky has to mix up with on the block," he whispered to his wife. "For God's sake, give her a nickel, give her some candy, give her anything, but let her run along."

Street child that I was, my instinct sensed the cold wave of his thought without hearing the exact words. Breaking away from Becky's detaining hand I made for the door.

"I want to go home! I want to go home!" I sobbed as I ran out of the room.

Whitman has said, "It is as lucky to die as it is to be born." And I put his thought into my own words, "It is as lucky not to have advantages as it is to have them." I mean that facing my disadvantages—the fears, the discouragements, the sense of inferiority—drove me to fight every inch of the way for things I demanded out of life. And, as a writer, the experience of forcing my way from the bottommost bottom gave me the knowledge of the poor that no well-born writer could possibly have.

I am thinking, for instance, of Victor Hugo and his immortal book, "Les Misérables." It's great literature, but it isn't the dirt and the blood of the poor that I saw and that forced me to write. Or take the American, Jack London: when he wrote about tramps he roused the sense of reality in his readers, because he had been a tramp. But later, when he tried to make stories of the great unwashed of the cities—again this was only literature.

The clear realization that literature is beyond my reach, that I must either be real or nothing, enables me to accept my place as the cobbler who must stick to his last, and gives my work any merit it may have. I stand on solid ground when I write of the poor, the homeless and the hungry.

Like many immigrants who expected to find America a realized Utopian dream, I had my disillusions. I quote here from an article which was published in *Good Housekeeping* in June, 1920.

When the editor told me that he would give me the chance to speak to the Americans out of my heart and say freely, not what I ought to feel—not what the Americans want me to feel—but what I actually do feel—something broke loose in me—a tightness that had held me strained like one whose fists are clenched—resisting—resisting——

Resisting what? Had I not come to America with open, outstretched arms, all my earthly possessions tied up in a handkerchief and all the hopes of humanity singing in my heart?

Had I not come to join hands with all those thousands of dreamers who had gone before me in search of the Golden Land? As I rushed forward with hungry eagerness to meet the expected welcoming, the very earth danced under my feet. All that I was, all that I had, I held out in my bare hands to America, the beloved, the prayed-for land.

But no hand was held out to meet mine. My eyes burned with longing—seeking—seeking for a comprehending glance. Where are the dreamers? cried my heart. My hands dropped down, my gifts unwanted.

I found no dreamers in America. I found rich men, poor men, educated men, ignorant men—struggling—all struggling—for bread, for rent, for banks, for mines. Rich and poor, educated and ignorant—straining—straining—wearing out their bodies, their brains, for the possession of things—money, power, position—their dreams forgotten.

I found in this rich land man still fighting man, as in the poorest part of the old country. Just as the starving Roumanian Jews, who had nothing to eat in their homeland but herring, when they became millionaires still ate herring from gold plates at banquets, so, throughout America, the dollar fight that grew up like a plague in times of poverty, killing the souls of men, still goes on in times of plenty.

I had expected to work in America, but work at the thing I loved—work with my mind, my heart, prepared for my work by education. I had dreamed of free schools, free colleges, where I could learn to give out my innermost thoughts and feelings to the world. But no sooner did I come off the ship than hunger drove me to the sweatshop, to become a "hand"—not a brain—not a soul—not a spirit—but just a "hand"—cramped, deadened into a part of a machine—a hand fit only to grasp, not to give.

Time came when I was able to earn my bread and rent. I earned what would have been wealth to me in Poland. My knotted nerves relaxed. I begun to breathe like a free human being. Ach! Maybe I could yet be at home in America. Maybe I could yet make something of myself. My choked-in spirit revived. There was a new light in my eyes, new strength in my arms and fingers. New hopes, new dreams beckoned to me. Should I take a night course in college, or buy myself the much-longed-for books, or treat myself to a little vacation to have time to think?

Then the landlady came with the raise in rent. The loaf of bread that was five cents became ten. Milk that was eight cents a quart became eighteen. Shoes, clothes, everything doubled and tripled in price. I felt like one put on a rack—thumb-screws torturing my flesh—pay—pay—pay!

What had been enough to give me comfort yesterday became starvation to-day. Always the cost of living leaping over the rise in wages. Never free from poverty—even in America.

And then I clenched my hands and swore that I would hold my dream of America—and fight for it. I refuse to accept the America where men make other men poor—create poverty where God has poured out wealth. I refuse to accept the America that gives the landlord the right to keep on raising my rent and to drive me to the streets when I do not earn enough to meet his rapacious demands.

I cry out in this wilderness for America—my America—different from all other countries. In this America promised to the oppressed of all lands, there is enough so that man need not fight man for his bread, but work with man, building the beauty that for hundreds of years, in thousands of starved villages of Europe, men have dreamed was America—beautiful homes—beautiful cities—beautiful lives reaching up for higher, ever higher visions of beauty.

I know you will say what right have I to come here and make demands upon America. But are not my demands the breath, the very life of America? What, after all, is America, but the response to the demands of immigrants like me, seeking new worlds in which their spirits may be free to create beauty? Were not the Pilgrim Fathers immigrants demanding a new world in which they could be free to live higher lives?

Yes, I make demands—not in arrogance, but in all humility. I demand—driven by my desire to give. I want to give not only that which I am, but that which I might be if I only had the chance. I want to give to America not the immigrant you see before you—starved, stunted, resentful, on the verge of hysteria from repression. I want to give a new kind of immigrant, full grown in mind and body—loving, serving, upholding America.

By writing out my protests and disillusions, I aired and clarified them. Slowly, I began to understand my unreasoning demands upon America and what America had to offer. I saw that America was a new world in the making, that anyone who has something real in him can find a way to contribute himself in this new world. But I saw I had to fight for my chance to give what I had to give, with the same life-and-death earnestness with which a man fights for his bread.

What had I with my empty hands and my hungry heart to give to America? I had my hunger, my homelessness, my dumbness, my blind searchings and gropings for what I knew not. I had to give to America my aching ignorance, my burning desire for knowledge. I had to give to America the dirt and the ugliness of my black life of poverty and my all-consuming passion for beauty.

As long as I kept stretching out my hands begging, begging for others to understand me, for friendship, for help—as long as I kept begging them to give me something—so long I was shut out from America. But the moment I understood America well enough to tell her about herself as I saw her— the moment I began to express myself—America accepted my self-expression as a gift from me, and from everywhere hands reached out to help me.

With the money I earned writing out stories of myself and my people, I was enabled to go abroad and to take another look around the Old World. I travelled from city to city. My special purpose was to talk to the poor people in the different countries and see how their chance to live compared with the chances of those in America.

I find that in no other country has the new-comer such a *direct* chance to come to the front and become a partner in the making of the country. Not where you come from, but what is in you and what you are, counts in America.

In no other country is there such healthy rebellion, such vital discontent, as there is among the poor in America. And the rebellion and discontent of the poor is in proportion to how well off they are. The poor people demand more of America than they ever dared to demand of their homeland, because America is brimming over with riches enough for everybody.

Life in America is a swift, sharp adventure. In the old countries things are more or less settled. In America the soil is young, and the people are young blossoming shoots of a new-grown civilization.

The writers of Europe can only be stylists, because life and traditions are fixed with them. In America life is yet unexplored, and lived new by each new-comer. And that is why America is such virgin stuff for the novelist.

Fiction is a mirror of life as it is being lived at the moment. And the moments are more static in Europe than in America. I admit that art is not so good in America as in Europe, because art is a decoration, and America is a young country too turbulent with life to take time to decorate itself.

I who used to be the most violent rebel of an immigrant, I now find myself the most ardent defender of America. I see every flaw of America perhaps more clearly than ever before. I know the ruthless commercialism of our big cities, the grabbing greed of landlords since the war making the thought of home almost impossible to the poor. I know that the gospel of success which rules in America hurts itself, because failure and defeat have revelations for humanity's deeper growth, to which success is deaf and dumb and blind.

I know how often the artists, the makers of beauty, in America are driven to the wall by the merciless extortion of those who sell the means of existence. But I know, too, that those of the artists who survive are vitalized by the killing things which had failed to kill them. America has no place for the dawdling, soft-spined, make-believe artists that swarm in the Paris cafés.

In the sunshine of the opportunities that have come to me, I am always aware of those around me and behind me who lacked the terrific vitality, the brutal self-absorption with which I had to fight for my chance or be blotted out. My eyes will always turn back with loneliness and longing for the old faces and old scenes that I loved more than my life. But though it tears my heart out of my body to go on, I must go on.

There's no going back to the Old World for anyone who has breathed the invigorating air of America. I return to America with the new realization that in no other country would a nobody from nowhere—one of the millions of lonely immigrants that pour through Ellis Island—a dumb thing with nothing but hunger and desire, get the chance to become articulate that America has given me.

CHILDREN OF LONELINESS

§ 1

"Oh, mother, can't you use a fork?" exclaimed Rachel as Mrs. Ravinsky took the shell of the baked potato in her fingers and raised it to her watering mouth.

"Here, *teacherin* mine, you want to learn me in my old age how to put the bite in my mouth?" The mother dropped the potato back into her plate, too wounded to eat. Wiping her hands on her blue-checked apron, she turned her glance to her husband, at the opposite side of the table.

"Yankev," she said bitterly, "stick your bone on a fork. Our *teacherin* said you dassn't touch no eatings with the hands."

"All my teachers died already in the old country," retorted the old man. "I ain't going to learn nothing new no more from my American daughter." He continued to suck the marrow out of the bone with that noisy relish that was so exasperating to Rachel.

"It's no use," stormed the girl, jumping up from the table in disgust; "I'll never be able to stand it here with you people."

"'You people'? What do you mean by 'you people'?" shouted the old man, lashed into fury by his daughter's words. "You think you got a different skin from us because you went to college?"

"It drives me wild to hear you crunching bones like savages. If you people won't change, I shall have to move and live by myself."

Yankev Ravinsky threw the half-gnawed bone upon the table with such vehemence that a plate broke into fragments.

"You witch you!" he cried in a hoarse voice tense with rage. "Move by yourself! We lived without you while you was away in college, and we can get on without you further. God ain't going to turn his nose on us because we ain't got table manners from America. A hell she made from this house since she got home."

"*Shah!* Yankev *leben*," pleaded the mother, "the neighbours are opening the windows to listen to our hollering. Let us have a little quiet for a while till the eating is over."

But the accumulated hurts and insults that the old man had borne in the one week since his daughter's return from college had reached the breaking-point. His face was convulsed, his eyes flashed, and his lips were flecked with froth as he burst out in a volley of scorn:

"You think you can put our necks in a chain and learn us new tricks? You think you can make us over for Americans? We got through till fifty years of our lives eating in our own old way——"

"Woe is me, Yankev *leben*!" entreated his wife. "Why can't we choke ourselves with our troubles? Why must the whole world know how we are tearing ourselves by the heads? In all Essex Street, in all New York, there ain't such fights like by us."

Her pleadings were in vain. There was no stopping Yankev Ravinsky once his wrath was roused. His daughter's insistence upon the use of a knife and fork spelled apostasy, anti-Semitism, and the aping of the gentiles.

Like a prophet of old condemning unrighteousness, he ran the gamut of denunciation, rising to heights of fury that were sublime and godlike, and sinking from sheer exhaustion to abusive bitterness.

"*Pfui* on all your American colleges! *Pfui* on the morals of America! No respect for old age. No fear for God. Stepping with your feet on all the laws of the holy Torah. A fire should burn out the whole new generation. They should sink into the earth, like Korah."

"Look at him cursing and burning! Just because I insist on their changing their terrible table manners. One would think I was killing them."

"Do you got to use a gun to kill?" cried the old man, little red threads darting out of the whites of his eyes.

"Who is doing the killing? Aren't you choking the life out of me? Aren't you dragging me by the hair to the darkness of past ages every minute of the day? I'd die of shame if one of my college friends should open the door while you people are eating."

"You—you——"

The old man was on the point of striking his daughter when his wife seized the hand he raised.

"*Mincha!* Yankev, you forgot *Mincha*!"

This reminder was a flash of inspiration on Mrs. Ravinsky's part, the only thing that could have ended the quarrelling instantly. *Mincha* was the prayer just before sunset of the orthodox Jews. This religious rite was so automatic with the old man that at his wife's mention of *Mincha* everything was immediately shut out, and Yankev Ravinsky rushed off to a corner of the room to pray.

"*Ashrai Yoishwai Waisahuh!*

"Happy are they who dwell in Thy house. Ever shall I praise Thee. *Selah!* Great is the Lord, and exceedingly to be praised; and His greatness is unsearchable. On the majesty and glory of Thy splendour, and on Thy marvellous deeds, will I meditate."

The shelter from the storms of life that the artist finds in his art, Yankev Ravinsky found in his prescribed communion with God. All the despair caused by his daughter's apostasy, the insults and disappointments he suffered, were in his sobbing voice. But as he entered into the spirit of his prayer, he felt the man of flesh drop away in the outflow of God around him. His voice mellowed, the rigid wrinkles of his face softened, the hard glitter of anger and condemnation in his eyes was transmuted into the light of love as he went on:

"The Lord is gracious and merciful; slow to anger and of great loving-kindness. To all that call upon Him in truth He will hear their cry and save them."

Oblivious to the passing and repassing of his wife as she warmed anew the unfinished dinner, he continued:

"Put not your trust in princes, in the son of man in whom there is no help." Here Reb Ravinsky paused long enough to make a silent confession for the sin of having placed his hope on his daughter instead of on God. His whole body bowed with the sense of guilt. Then in a moment his humility was transfigured into exaltation. Sorrow for sin dissolved in joy as he became more deeply aware of God's unfailing protection.

"Happy is he who hath the God of Jacob for his help, whose hope is in the Lord his God. He healeth the broken in heart, and bindeth up their wounds."

A healing balm filled his soul as he returned to the table, where the steaming hot food awaited him. Rachel sat near the window pretending to read a book. Her mother did not urge her to join them at the table, fearing another outbreak, and the meal continued in silence.

The girl's thoughts surged hotly as she glanced from her father to her mother. A chasm of four centuries could not have separated her more completely from them than her four years at Cornell.

"To think that I was born of these creatures! It's an insult to my soul. What kinship have I with these two lumps of ignorance and superstition? They're ugly and gross and stupid. I'm all sensitive nerves. They want to wallow in dirt."

She closed her eyes to shut out the sight of her parents as they silently ate together, unmindful of the dirt and confusion.

"How is it possible that I lived with them and like them only four years ago? What is it in me that so quickly gets accustomed to the best? Beauty and cleanliness are as natural to me as if I'd been born on Fifth Avenue instead of in the dirt of Essex Street."

A vision of Frank Baker passed before her. Her last long talk with him out under the trees in college still lingered in her heart. She felt that she had only to be with him again to carry forward the beautiful friendship that had sprung up between them. He had promised to come shortly to New York. How could she possibly introduce such a born and bred American to her low, ignorant, dirty parents?

"I might as well tear the thought of Frank Baker out of my heart," she told herself. "If he just once sees the pigsty of a home I come from, if he just sees the table manners of my father and mother, he'll fly through the ceiling."

Timidly, Mrs. Ravinsky turned to her daughter.

"Ain't you going to give a taste the eating?"

No answer.

"I fried the *lotkes* special for you——"

"I can't stand your fried, greasy stuff."

"Ain't even my cooking good no more neither?" Her gnarled, hard-worked hands clutched at her breast. "God from the world, for what do I need yet any more my life? Nothing I do for my child is no use no more."

Her head sank; her whole body seemed to shrivel and grow old with the sense of her own futility.

"How I was hurrying to run by the butcher before everybody else, so as to pick out the grandest, fattest piece of *brust*!" she wailed, tears streaming down her face. "And I put my hand away from my heart and put a whole fresh egg into the *lotkes*, and I stuffed the stove full of coal like a millionaire so as to get the *lotkes* fried so nice and brown; and now you give a kick on everything I done——"

"Fool woman," shouted her husband, "stop laying yourself on the ground for your daughter to step on you! What more can you expect from a child raised up in America? What more can you expect but that she should spit in your face and make dirt from you?" His eyes, hot and dry under their lids, flashed from his wife to his daughter. "The old Jewish eating is poison to her; she must have *treifah* ham—only forbidden food."

Bitter laughter shook him.

"Woman, how you patted yourself with pride before all the neighbours, boasting of our great American daughter coming home from college! This is our daughter, our pride, our hope, our pillow for our old age that we were dreaming about. This is our American *teacherin*! A Jew-hater, an anti-Semite we brought into the world, a betrayer of our race who hates her own father and mother like the Russian Tsar once hated a Jew. She makes herself so refined, she can't stand it when we use the knife or fork the wrong way; but her heart is that of a brutal Cossack, and she spills her own father's and mother's blood like water."

Every word he uttered seared Rachel's soul like burning acid. She felt herself becoming a witch, a she-devil, under the spell of his accusations.

"You want me to love you yet?" She turned upon her father like an avenging fury. "If there's any evil hatred in my soul, you have roused it with your cursed preaching."

"*Oi-i-i!* Highest One! pity Yourself on us!" Mrs. Ravinsky wrung her hands. "Rachel, Yankev, let there be an end to this knife-stabbing! *Gottuniu!* my flesh is torn to pieces!"

Unheeding her mother's pleading, Rachel rushed to the closet where she kept her things.

"I was a crazy idiot to think that I could live with you people under one roof." She flung on her hat and coat and bolted for the door.

Mrs. Ravinsky seized Rachel's arm in passionate entreaty.

"My child, my heart, my life, what do you mean? Where are you going?"

"I mean to get out of this hell of a home this very minute," she said, tearing loose from her mother's clutching hands.

"Woe is me! My child! We'll be to shame and to laughter by the whole world. What will people say?"

"Let them say! My life is my own; I'll live as I please." She slammed the door in her mother's face.

"They want me to love them yet," ran the mad thoughts in Rachel's brain as she hurried through the streets, not knowing where she was going, not caring. "Vampires, bloodsuckers fastened on my flesh! Black shadow blighting every ray of light that ever came my way! Other parents scheme and plan and wear themselves out to give their child a chance, but they put dead stones in front of every chance I made for myself."

With the cruelty of youth to everything not youth, Rachel reasoned:

"They have no rights, no claims over me, like other parents who do things for their children. It was my own brains, my own courage, my own iron will that forced my way out of the sweatshop to my present position in the public schools. I owe them nothing, nothing, nothing."

§ 2

Two weeks already away from home, Rachel looked about her room. It was spotlessly clean. She had often said to herself while at home with her parents: "All I want is an empty room, with a bed and table and chair. As long as it is clean and away from them, I'll be happy."

But was she happy?

A distant door closed, followed by the retreating sound of descending footsteps. Then all was still, the stifling stillness of a lodging-house. The white, empty walls pressed in upon her, suffocated her. She listened acutely for any stir of life, but the continued silence was unbroken save for the insistent ticking of her watch.

"I ran away from home burning for life," she mused, "and all I've found is the loneliness that's death." A wave of self-pity weakened her almost to the point of tears. "I'm alone! I'm alone!" she moaned, crumpling into a heap.

"Must it always be with me like this," her soul cried in terror, "either to live among those who drag me down or in the awful isolation of a hall bed-room? Oh, I'll die of loneliness among these frozen, each-shut-in-himself Americans! It's one thing to break away, but, oh, the strength to go on alone! How can I ever do it? The love instinct is so strong in me; I cannot live without love, without people."

The thought of a letter from Frank Baker suddenly lightened her spirits. That very evening she was to meet him for dinner. Here was hope, more than hope. Just seeing him again would surely bring the certainty.

This new rush of light upon her dark horizon so softened her heart that she could almost tolerate her superfluous parents.

"If I could only have love and my own life, I could almost forgive them for bringing me into the world. I don't really hate them; I only hate them when they stand between me and the new America that I'm to conquer."

Answering her impulse, her feet led her to the familiar Ghetto streets. On the corner of the block where her parents lived she paused, torn between the desire to see her people and the fear of their nagging reproaches. The old

Jewish proverb came to her mind: "The wolf is not afraid of the dog, but he hates his bark." "I'm not afraid of their black curses for sin. It's nothing to me if they accuse me of being an anti-Semite or a murderer, and yet why does it hurt me so?"

Rachel had prepared herself to face the usual hail-storm of reproaches and accusations, but as she entered the dark hallway of the tenement, she heard her father's voice chanting the old familiar Hebrew psalm of "The Race of Sorrows":

"Hear my prayer, O Lord, and let my cry come unto Thee.

"For my days are consumed like smoke, and my bones are burned as an hearth.

"I am like a pelican of the wilderness.

"I am like an owl of the desert.

"I have eaten ashes like bread and mingled my drink with weeping."

A faintness came over her. The sobbing strains of the lyric song melted into her veins like a magic sap, making her warm and human again. All her strength seethed to flow out of her in pity for her people. She longed to throw herself on the dirty, ill-smelling tenement stairs and weep: "Nothing is real but love—love. Nothing so false as ambition."

Since her early childhood she remembered often waking up in the middle of the night and hearing her father chant this age-old song of woe. There flashed before her a vivid picture of him, huddled in the corner beside the table piled high with Hebrew books, swaying to the rhythm of his jeremiad, the sputtering light of the candle stuck in a bottle throwing uncanny shadows over his gaunt face. The skull-cap, the side-locks, and the long grey beard made him seem like some mystic stranger from a far-off world and not a father. The father of the daylight who ate with a knife, spat on the floor, and who was forever denouncing America and Americans was different from this stranger of the mystic spirit who could thrill with such impassioned rapture.

Thousands of years of exile, thousands of years of hunger, loneliness, and want swept over her as she listened to her father's voice. Something seemed to be crying out to her to run in and seize her father and mother in her arms and hold them close.

"Love, love—nothing is true between us but love," she thought.

But why couldn't she do what she longed to do? Why, with all her passionate sympathy for them, should any actual contact with her people seem so impossible? No, she couldn't go in just yet. Instead, she ran up on the roof, where she could be alone. She stationed herself at the air-shaft opposite their kitchen window, where for the first time since she had left in a rage she could see her old home.

Ach! what sickening disorder! In the sink were the dirty dishes stacked high, untouched, it looked, for days. The table still held the remains of the last meal. Clothes were strewn about the chairs. The bureau-drawers were open, and their contents brimmed over in mad confusion.

"I couldn't endure it, this terrible dirt!" Her nails dug into her palms, shaking with the futility of her visit. "It would be worse than death to go back to them. It would mean giving up order, cleanliness, sanity, everything that I've striven all these years to attain. It would mean giving up the hope of my new world—the hope of Frank Baker."

The sound of the creaking door reached her where she crouched against the air-shaft. She looked again into the murky depths of the room. Her mother had entered. With arms full of paper bags of provisions, the old woman paused on the threshold, her eyes dwelling on the dim figure of her husband. A look of pathetic tenderness illumined her wrinkled features.

"I'll make something good to eat for you, yes?"

Reb Ravinsky only dropped his head on his breast. His eyes were red and dry, sandy with sorrow that could find no release in tears. Good God! never had Rachel seen such profound despair. For the first time she noticed the grooved tracings of withering age knotted on his face and the growing hump on her mother's back.

"Already the shadow of death hangs over them," she thought as she watched them. "They're already with one foot in the grave. Why can't I be human to them before they're dead? Why can't I?"

Rachel blotted away the picture of the sordid room with both hands over her eyes.

"To death with my soul! I wish I were a plain human being with a heart instead of a monster of selfishness with a soul."

But the pity she felt for her parents began now to be swept away in a wave of pity for herself.

"How every step in advance costs me my heart's blood! My greatest tragedy in life is that I always see the two opposite sides at the same time. What seems to me right one day seems all wrong the next. Not only that, but many things seem right and wrong at the same time. I feel I have a right to my own life, and yet I feel just as strongly that I owe my father and mother something. Even if I don't love them, I have no right to step over them. I'm drawn to them by something more compelling than love. It is the cry of their dumb, wasted lives."

Again Rachel looked into the dimly lighted room below. Her mother placed food upon the table. With a self-effacing stoop of humility, she entreated, "Eat only while it is hot yet."

With his eyes fixed almost unknowingly, Reb Ravinsky sat down. Her mother took the chair opposite him, but she only pretended to eat the slender portion of the food she had given herself.

Rachel's heart swelled. Yes, it had always been like that. Her mother had taken the smallest portion of everything for herself. Complaints, reproaches, upbraidings, abuse, yes, all these had been heaped by her upon her mother; but always the juiciest piece of meat was placed on her plate, the thickest slice of bread; the warmest covering was given to her, while her mother shivered through the night.

"Ah, I don't want to abandon them!" she thought; "I only want to get to the place where I belong. I only want to get to the mountain-tops and view the world from the heights, and then I'll give them everything I've achieved."

Her thoughts were sharply broken in upon by the loud sound of her father's eating. Bent over the table, he chewed with noisy gulps a piece of herring, his temples working to the motion of his jaws. With each audible swallow and smacking of the lips, Rachel's heart tightened with loathing.

"Their dirty ways turn all my pity into hate." She felt her toes and her fingers curl inward with disgust. "I'll never amount to anything if I'm not strong enough to break away from them once and for all." Hypnotizing herself into her line of self-defence, her thoughts raced on: "I'm only cruel to be kind. If I went back to them now, it would not be out of love, but because of weakness—because of doubt and unfaith in myself."

Rachel bluntly turned her back. Her head lifted. There was iron will in her jaws.

"If I haven't the strength to tear free from the old, I can never conquer the new. Every new step a man makes is a tearing away from those clinging to him. I must get tight and hard as rock inside of me if I'm ever to do the things I set out to do. I must learn to suffer and suffer, walk through blood and fire, and not bend from my course."

For the last time she looked at her parents. The terrible loneliness of their abandoned old age, their sorrowful eyes, the wrung-dry weariness on their faces, the whole black picture of her ruined, desolate home, burned into her flesh. She knew all the pain of one unjustly condemned, and the guilt of one with the spilt blood of helpless lives upon his hands. Then came tears, blinding, wrenching tears that tore at her heart until it seemed that they would rend her body into shreds.

"God! God!" she sobbed as she turned her head away from them, "if all this suffering were at least for something worth while, for something outside myself! But to have to break them and crush them merely because I have a fastidious soul that can't stomach their table manners, merely because I can't strangle my aching ambitions to rise in the world!"

She could no longer sustain the conflict which raged within her higher and higher at every moment. With a sudden tension of all her nerves she pulled herself together and stumbled blindly down the stairs and out of the house. And she felt as if she had torn away from the flesh and blood of her own body.

§ 3

Out in the street she struggled to get hold of herself again. Despite the tumult and upheaval that racked her soul, an intoxicating lure still held her up—the hope of seeing Frank Baker that evening. She was indeed a storm-racked ship, but within sight of shore. She need but throw out the signal, and help was nigh. She need but confide to Frank Baker of her break with her people, and all the dormant sympathy between them would surge up. His understanding would widen and deepen because of her great need for his understanding. He would love her the more because of her great need for his love.

Forcing back her tears, stepping over her heartbreak, she hurried to the hotel where she was to meet him. Her father's impassioned rapture when he chanted the psalms of David lit up the visionary face of the young Jewess.

"After all, love is the beginning of the real life," she thought as Frank Baker's dark, handsome face flashed before her. "With him to hold on to, I'll begin my new world."

Borne higher and higher by the intoxicating illusion of her great destiny, she cried:

"A person all alone is but a futile cry in an unheeding wilderness. One alone is but a shadow, an echo of reality. It takes two together to create reality. Two together can pioneer a new world."

With a vision of herself and Frank Baker marching side by side to the conquest of her heart's desire, she added:

"No wonder a man's love means so little to the American woman. They belong to the world in which they are born. They belong to their fathers and mothers; they belong to their relatives and friends. They are human even without a man's love. I don't belong; I'm not human. Only a man's love can save me and make me human again."

It was the busy dinner-hour at the fashionable restaurant. Pausing at the doorway with searching eyes and lips eagerly parted, Rachel's swift glance circled the lobby. Those seated in the dining-room beyond who were not too absorbed in one another, noticed a slim, vivid figure of ardent youth, but with dark, age-old eyes that told of the restless seeking of her homeless race.

With nervous little movements of anxiety, Rachel sat down, got up, then started across the lobby. Half-way, she stopped, and her breath caught.

"Mr. Baker," she murmured, her hands fluttering toward him with famished eagerness. His smooth, athletic figure had a cocksureness that to the girl's worshipping gaze seemed the perfection of male strength.

"You must be doing wonderful things," came from her admiringly, "you look so happy, so shining with life."

"Yes"—he shook her hand vigorously—"I've been living for the first time since I was a kid. I'm full of such interesting experiences. I'm actually working in an East Side settlement."

Dazed by his glamorous success, Rachel stammered soft phrases of congratulation as he led her to a table. But seated opposite him, the face of this untried youth, flushed with the health and happiness of another world than that of the poverty-crushed Ghetto, struck her almost as an insincerity.

"You in an East Side settlement?" she interrupted sharply. "What reality can there be in that work for you?"

"Oh," he cried, his shoulders squaring with the assurance of his master's degree in sociology, "it's great to get under the surface and see how the other half live. It's so picturesque! My conception of these people has greatly changed since I've been visiting their homes." He launched into a glowing account of the East Side as seen by a twenty-five-year-old college graduate.

"I thought them mostly immersed in hard labour, digging subways or slaving in sweatshops," he went on. "But think of the poetry which the immigrant is daily living!"

"But they're so sunk in the dirt of poverty, what poetry do you see there?"

"It's their beautiful home life, the poetic devotion between parents and children, the sacrifices they make for one another——"

"Beautiful home life? Sacrifices? Why, all I know of is the battle to the knife between parents and children. It's black tragedy that boils there, not the pretty sentiments that you imagine."

"My dear child"—he waved aside her objection—"you're too close to judge dispassionately. This very afternoon, on one of my friendly visits, I came upon a dear old man who peered up at me through horn-rimmed glasses behind his pile of Hebrew books. He was hardly able to speak English, but I found him a great scholar."

"Yes, a lazy old do-nothing, a bloodsucker on his wife and children."

Too shocked for remonstrance, Frank Baker stared at her.

"How else could he have time in the middle of the afternoon to pore over his books?" Rachel's voice was hard with bitterness. "Did you see his wife? I'll bet she was slaving for him in the kitchen. And his children slaving for him in the sweatshop."

"Even so, think of the fine devotion that the women and children show in making the lives of your Hebrew scholars possible. It's a fine contribution to America, where our tendency is to forget idealism."

"Give me better a plain American man who supports his wife and children, and I'll give you all those dreamers of the Talmud."

He smiled tolerantly at her vehemence.

"Nevertheless," he insisted, "I've found wonderful material for my new book in all this. I think I've got a new angle on the social types of your East Side."

An icy band tightened about her heart. "Social types," her lips formed. How could she possibly confide to this man of the terrible tragedy that she had been through that very day? Instead of the understanding and sympathy that she had hoped to find, there were only smooth platitudes, the sight-seer's surface interest in curious "social types."

Frank Baker talked on. Rachel seemed to be listening, but her eyes had a far-off, abstracted look. She was quiet as a spinning-top is quiet, her thoughts and emotions revolving within her at high speed.

"That man in love with me? Why, he doesn't see me or feel me. I don't exist to him. He's only stuck on himself, blowing his own horn. Will he never stop with his 'I,' 'I,' 'I'? Why, I was a crazy lunatic to think that just because we took the same courses in college he would understand me out in the real world."

All the fire suddenly went out of her eyes. She looked a thousand years old as she sank back wearily in her chair.

"Oh, but I'm boring you with all my heavy talk on sociology." Frank Baker's words seemed to come to her from afar. "I have tickets for a fine musical comedy that will cheer you up, Miss Ravinsky——"

"Thanks, thanks," she cut in hurriedly. Spend a whole evening sitting beside him in a theatre when her heart was breaking? No. All she wanted was to get away—away where she could be alone. "I have work to do," she heard herself say. "I've got to get home."

Frank Baker murmured words of polite disappointment and escorted her back to her door. She watched the sure swing of his athletic figure as he strode away down the street, then she rushed upstairs.

Back in her little room, stunned, bewildered, blinded with her disillusion, she sat staring at her four empty walls.

Hours passed, but she made no move, she uttered no sound. Doubled fists thrust between her knees, she sat there, staring blindly at her empty walls.

"I can't live with the old world, and I'm yet too green for the new. I don't belong to those who gave me birth or to those with whom I was educated."

Was this to be the end of all her struggles to rise in America, she asked herself, this crushing daze of loneliness? Her driving thirst for an education, her desperate battle for a little cleanliness, for a breath of beauty, the tearing away from her own flesh and blood to free herself from the yoke of her parents—what was it all worth now? Where did it lead to? Was loneliness to be the fruit of it all?

Night was melting away like a fog; through the open window the first lights of dawn were appearing. Rachel felt the sudden touch of the sun upon her face, which was bathed in tears. Overcome by her sorrow, she shuddered and put her hand over her eyes as though to shut out the unwelcome contact. But the light shone through her fingers.

Despite her weariness, the renewing breath of the fresh morning entered her heart like a sunbeam. A mad longing for life filled her veins.

"I want to live," her youth cried. "I want to live, even at the worst."

Live how? Live for what? She did not know. She only felt she must struggle against her loneliness and weariness as she had once struggled against dirt, against the squalor and ugliness of her Ghetto home.

Turning from the window, she concentrated her mind, her poor tired mind, on one idea.

"I have broken away from the old world; I'm through with it. It's already behind me. I must face this loneliness till I get to the new world. Frank Baker can't help me; I must hope for no help from the outside. I'm alone; I'm alone till I get there.

"But am I really alone in my seeking? I'm one of the millions of immigrant children, children of loneliness, wandering between worlds that are at once too old and too new to live in."

BROTHERS

I had just begun to unpack and arrange my things in my new quarters when Hanneh Breineh edged herself confidingly into my room and started to tell me the next chapter in the history of all her lodgers.

"And this last one what sleeps in the kitchen," she finished, "he's such a stingy—Moisheh the Schnorrer they call him. He washes himself his own shirts and sews together the holes from his socks to save a penny. Think only! He cooks himself his own meat once a week for the Sabbath and the rest of the time it's cabbage and potatoes or bread and herring. And the herring what he buys are the squashed and smashed ones from the bottom of the barrel. And the bread he gets is so old and hard he's got to break it with a hammer. For why should such a stingy grouch live in this world if he don't allow himself the bite in the mouth?"

It was no surprise to me that Hanneh Breineh knew all this, for everybody in her household cooked and washed in the same kitchen, and everybody knew what everybody else ate and what everybody else wore down to the number of patches on their underwear.

"And by what do you work for a living?" she asked, as she settled herself on my cot.

"I study at college by day and I give English lessons and write letters for the people in the evening."

"Ach! So you are learning for a *teacherin*?" She rose, and looked at me up and down and down and up, her red-lidded eyes big with awe. "So that's why you wanted so particular a room to yourself? Nobody in my house has a room by herself alone just like you. They all got to squeeze themselves together to make it come out cheaper."

By the evening everybody in that house knew I was a *teacherin*, and Moisheh the Schnorrer was among my first applicants for instruction.

"How much will you charge me for learning me English, a lesson?" he blurted, abrupt because of his painful bashfulness.

I looked up at the tall, ungainly creature with round, stooping shoulders, and massive, shaggy head—physically a veritable giant, yet so timid, so diffident, afraid almost of his own shadow.

"I wanna learn how to sign myself my name," he went on. "Only—you'll make it for me a little cheaper—yes?"

"Fifty cents an hour," I answered, drawn by the dumb, hunted look that cried to me out of his eyes.

Moisheh scratched his shaggy head and bit the nails of his huge, toil-worn hand. "Maybe—could you yet—perhaps—make it a little cheaper?" he fumbled.

"Aren't you working?"

His furrowed face coloured with confusion. "Yes—but—but my family. I got to save myself together a penny to a penny for them."

"Oh! So you're already married?"

"No—not married. My family in Russia—*mein* old mother and Feivel, *mein* doctor brother, and Berel the baby, he was already learning for a book-keeper before the war."

The coarse peasant features were transformed with tenderness as he started to tell me the story of his loved ones in Russia.

"Seven years ago I came to America. I thought only to make quick money to send the ship tickets for them all, but I fell into the hands of a cockroach boss.

"You know a cockroach boss is a *landsman* that comes to meet the greenhorns by the ship. He made out he wanted to help me, but he only wanted to sweat me into my grave. Then came the war and I began to earn big wages; but they were driven away from their village and my money didn't get to them at all. And for more than a year I didn't know if my people were yet alive in the world."

He took a much-fingered, greasy envelope from his pocket. "That's the first letter I got from them in months. The book-keeper boarder read it for me already till he's sick from it. Only read it for me over again," he begged as he handed it to me upside down.

The letter was from Smirsk, Poland, where the two brothers and their old mother had fled for refuge. It was the cry of despair—food—clothes—shoes—the cry of hunger and nakedness. His eyes filled and unheeding tears fell on his rough, trembling hands as I read.

"That I should have bread three times a day and them starving!" he gulped. "By each bite it chokes me. And when I put myself on my warm coat, it shivers in me when I think how they're without a shirt on their backs. I already sent them a big package of things, but until I hear from them I'm like without air in my lungs."

I wondered how, in their great need and in his great anxiety to supply it, he could think of English lessons or spare the little money to pay for his tuition.

He divined my thoughts. "Already seven years I'm here and I didn't take for myself the time to go night school," he explained. "Now they'll come soon and I don't want them to shame themselves from their *Amerikaner* brother what can't sign his own name, and they in Russia write me such smart letters in English."

"Didn't you go to school like your brothers?"

"Me—school?" He shrugged his toil-stooped shoulders. "I was the only breadgiver after my father he died. And with my nose in the earth on a farm how could I take myself the time to learn?"

His queer, bulging eyes with their yearning, passionate look seemed to cling to something beyond—out of reach. "But my brothers—*ach*! my brothers! They're so high-educated! I worked the nails from off my fingers, but only they should learn—they should become people in the world."

And he deluged me with questions as to the rules of immigrant admission and how long it would take for him to learn to sign his name so that he would be a competent leader when his family would arrive.

"I ain't so dumb like I look on my face." He nudged me confidentially. "I already found out from myself which picture means where the train goes. If it's for Brooklyn Bridge, then the hooks go this way"—he clumsily drew in the air with his thick fingers—"and if it's for the South Ferry, then the words twist the other way around."

I marvelled at his frank revelation of himself.

"What is your work?" I asked, more and more drawn by some hidden power of this simple peasant.

"I'm a presser by pants."

Now I understood the cause of the stooped, rounded shoulders. It must have come from pounding away with a heavy iron at an ironing board, day after day, year after year. But for all the ravages of poverty, of mean, soul-crushing drudgery that marked this man, something big and indomitable in him fascinated me. His was the strength knitted and knotted from the hardiest roots of the earth. Filled with awe, I looked up at him. Here was a man submerged in the darkness of illiteracy—of pinch and scraping and want— yet untouched—unspoiled, with the same simplicity of spirit that was his as a wide-eyed, dreamy youth in the green fields of Russia.

We had our first lesson, and, though I needed every cent I could earn, I felt like a thief taking his precious pennies. But he would pay. "It's worth to me more than a quarter only to learn how to hold up the pencil," he exulted as he gripped the pencil upright in his thick fist. All the yearning, the intense desire for education were in the big, bulging eyes that he raised towards me. "No wonder I could never make those little black hooks for words; I was always grabbing my pencil like a fork for sticking up meat."

With what sublime absorption he studied me as I showed him how to shape the letters for his name! Eyes wide—mouth open—his huge, stoop-shouldered body leaning forward—quivering with hunger to grasp the secret turnings of "the little black hooks" that signified his name.

"M-o-i-s-h-e-h," he repeated after me as I guided his pencil.

"Now do it alone," I urged.

Moisheh rolled up his sleeve like one ready for a fray. The sweat dripped from his face as he struggled for the muscular control of his clumsy fingers.

Night after night he wrestled heroically with the "little black hooks." At last his efforts were rewarded. He learned how to shape the letters without any help.

"God from the world!" he cried with childishly pathetic joy as he wrote his name for the first time. "This is me—Moisheh!" He lifted the paper and held it off and then held it close, drunk with the wonder of the "little black hooks." They seemed so mysterious to him, and his eyes loomed large—transfigured with the miracle of seeing himself for the first time in script.

It was the week after that he asked me to write his letter, and this time it was from my eyes that the unheeding tears dropped as I wrote the words he dictated.

"To my dear Loving Mother, and to my worthy Honourable Brother Feivel, the Doctor, and to my youngest brother, the joy from my life, the light from mine eyes, Berel the Book-keeper!

"Long years and good luck to you all. Thanks the highest One in Heaven that you are alive. Don't worry for nothing. So long I have yet my two strong hands to work you will yet live to have from everything plenty. For all those starving days in Russia, you will live to have joy in America.

"You, Feivel, will yet have a grand doctor's office, with an electric dentist sign over your door, and a gold tooth to pull in the richest customers. And you, Berel, my honourable book-keeper, will yet live to wear a white starched collar like all the higher-ups in America. And you, my loving mother, will yet shine up the block with the joy from your children.

"I am sending you another box of things, and so soon as I get from you the word, I'll send for you the ship tickets, even if it costs the money from all the banks in America.

"Luck and blessings on your dear heads. I am going around praying and counting the minutes till you are all with me together in America."

Our lessons had gone on steadily for some months and already he was able to write the letters of the alphabet. One morning before I was out of bed he knocked at my door.

"Quick only! A blue letter printed from Russia!" he shouted in an excited voice.

Through the crack of the door he shoved in the cablegram. "Send ship tickets or we die—pogrom," I read aloud.

"*Weh—weh!*" A cry of a dumb, wounded animal broke from the panic-stricken Moisheh.

The cup of coffee that Hanneh Breineh lifted to her lips dropped with a crash to the floor. "Where pogrom?" she demanded, rushing in.

I re-read the cablegram.

"Money for ship tickets!" stammered Moisheh. He drew forth a sweaty moneybag that lay hid beneath his torn grey shirt and with trembling hands began counting the greasy bills. "Only four hundred and thirty-three dollars! Woe is me!" He cracked the knuckles of his fingers in a paroxysm of grief. "It's six hundred I got to have!"

"*Gottuniu!* Listen to him only!" Hanneh Breineh shook Moisheh roughly. "You'd think he was living by wild Indians—not by people with hearts...."

"Boarders!" she called. "Moisheh's old mother and his two brothers are in Smirsk where there's a pogrom."

The word "pogrom" struck like a bombshell. From the sink, the stove, they gathered, in various stages of undress, around Moisheh, electrified into one bond of suffering brotherhood.

Hanneh Breineh, hand convulsively clutching her breast, began an impassioned appeal. "Which from us here needs me to tell what's a pogrom? It drips yet the blood from my heart when I only begin to remember. Only nine years old I was—the *pogromschiks* fell on our village.... Frightened!... You all know what's to be frightened from death—frightened from being burned alive or torn to pieces by wild wolves—but what's that compared to the cold shiverings that shook us by the hands and feet when we heard the drunken Cossacks coming nearer and nearer our hut. The last second my mother, like a crazy, pushed me and my little sister into the chimney. We heard the house tremble with shots—cries from my mother—father—then stillness. In the middle of the black night my little sister and I crawled ourselves out to see——" Hanneh Breineh covered her eyes as though to shut out the hideous vision.

Again Hanneh Breineh's voice arose. "I got no more breath for words—only this—the last bite from our mouths, the last shirt from our backs we got to take away to help out Moisheh. It's not only Moisheh's old mother that's out there—it's our own old mother—our own flesh-and-blood brothers.... Even I—beggar that I am—even I will give my only feather bed to the pawn."

A hush, and then a tumult of suppressed emotion. The room seethed with wild longings of the people to give—to help—to ease their aching hearts sharing Moisheh's sorrow.

Shoolem, a grey, tottering ragpicker, brought forth a grimy cigar-box full of change. "Here is all the pennies and nickels and dimes I was saving and saving myself for fifteen years. I was holding by life on one hope—the hope that some day I would yet die before the holy walls from Jerusalem." With the gesture of a Rothschild he waved it in the air as he handed it over. "But here you got it, Moisheh. May it help to bring your brothers in good luck to America!"

Sosheh, the finisher, turned aside as she dug into her stocking and drew forth a crisp five-dollar bill. "That all I got till my next pay. Only it should help them," she gulped. "I wish I had somebody left alive that I could send a ship ticket to."

Zaretsky, the matchmaker, snuffed noisily a pinch of tobacco and pulled from his overcoat pocket a book of War Savings stamps. "I got fourteen dollars of American Liberty. Only let them come in good luck and I'll fix them out yet with the two grandest girls in New York."

The ship bearing Moisheh's family was to dock the next morning at eleven o'clock. The night before Hanneh Breineh and all of us were busy decorating the house in honour of the arrivals. The sound of hammering and sweeping and raised, excited voices filled the air.

Sosheh, the finisher, standing on top of a soap box, was garnishing the chandelier with red-paper flowers.

Hanneh Breineh tacked bright, checked oilcloth on top of the washtubs.

Zaretsky was nailing together the broken leg of the table.

"I should live so," laughed Sosheh, her sallow face flushed with holiday joy. "This kitchen almost shines like a parlour, but for only this——" pointing to the sagging lounge where the stained mattress protruded.

"*Shah!* I'll fix this up in a minute so it'll look like new from the store." And Hanneh Breineh took out the red-flowered, Sabbath tablecloth from the bureau and tucked it around the lounge.

Meantime Moisheh, his eyes popping with excitement, raised clouds of dust as he swept dirt that had been gathering since Passover from the corners of the room.

Unable to wait any longer for the big moment, he had been secretly planning for weeks, zip! under the bed went the mountain of dirt, to be followed by the broom, which he kicked out of sight.

"Enough with the cleaning!" he commanded. "Come only around," and he pulled out from the corner his Russian steamer basket.

"Oi—oi—oi—oi, and ai—ai!" the boarders shouted, hilariously. "Will you treat us to a holiday cake maybe?"

"Wait only!" He gesticulated grandly as he loosened the lock.

One by one he held up and displayed the treasured trousseau which little by little he had gathered together for his loved ones.

A set of red-woollen underwear for each of the brothers, and for his mother a thick, grey shirt. Heavy cotton socks, a blue-checked apron, and a red-velvet waist appeared next. And then—Moisheh was reduced to guttural grunts of primitive joy as he unfolded a rainbow tie for Feivel, the doctor, and pink suspenders for his "baby" brother.

Moisheh did not remove his clothes—no sleep for him that night. It was still dark when the sound of his heavy shoes, clumping around the kitchen as he cooked his breakfast, woke the rest of us.

"You got to come with me—I can't hold myself together with so much joy," he implored. There was no evading his entreaties, so I promised to get away as soon as I could and meet him at the dock.

I arrived at Ellis Island to find Moisheh stamping up and down like a wild horse. "What are they holding them so long?" he cried, mad with anxiety to reach those for whom he had so long waited and hungered.

I had to shake him roughly before I could make him aware of my presence, and immediately he was again lost in his eager search of the mob that crowded the gates.

The faces of the immigrants, from the tiniest babe at its mother's breast to the most decrepit old grey-haired man, were all stamped with the same transfigured look—a look of those who gazed for the first time upon the radiance of the dawn. The bosoms of the women heaved with excitement. The men seemed to be expanding, growing with the surge of realized hopes, of dreams come true. They inhaled deeply, eager to fill their stifled bodies and souls with the first life-giving breath of free air. Their eyes were luminous with hope, bewildered joy and vague forebodings. A voice was heard above the shouted orders and shuffling feet—above the clamour of the pressing crowds—"*Gott sei dank!*" The pæan of thanksgiving was echoed and re-echoed—a pæan of nations released—America.

I had to hold tight to the bars not to be trampled underfoot by the crowd that surged through the gates. Suddenly a wild animal cry tore from Moisheh's throat. "*Mammeniu! Mammeniu!*" And a pair of gorilla-like arms infolded a gaunt, wasted little figure wrapped in a shawl.

"Moisheh! my heart!" she sobbed, devouring him with hunger-ravaged eyes.

"*Ach!*" She trembled—drawing back to survey her first-born. "From the bare feet and rags of Smirsk to leather shoes and a suit like a Rothschild!" she cried in Yiddish. "*Ach!*—I lived to see America!"

A dumb thing laughing and crying he stood there, a primitive figure, pathetic, yet sublime in the purity of his passionate love, his first love—his love for his mother.

The toil-worn little hand pulled at his neck as she whispered in Moisheh's ear, and as in a dream he turned with outstretched arms to greet his brothers.

"Feivel—*mein* doctor!" he cried.

"Yes, yes, we're here," said the high-browed young doctor in a tone that I thought was a little impatient. "Now let's divide up these bundles and get started." Moisheh's willing arms reached out for the heaviest sack.

"And here is my *teacherin!*" Moisheh's grin was that of a small boy displaying his most prized possession.

Berel, the baby, with the first down of young manhood still soft on his cheeks, shyly enveloped my hand in his long, sensitive fingers. "How nice for you to come—a *teacherin*—an *Amerikanerin!*"

"Well—are we going?" came imperiously from the doctor.

"Yeh—yeh!" answered Moisheh. "I'm so out of my head from joy, my feet don't work." And, gathering the few remaining lighter packages together, we threaded our way through the crowded streets—the two newly arrived brothers walking silently together.

"Has Moisheh changed much?" I asked the doctor as I watched the big man help his mother tenderly across the car tracks.

"The same Moisheh," he said, with an amused, slightly superior air.

I looked at Berel to see if he was of the same cloth as the doctor, but he was lost in dreamy contemplation of the towering sky-scrapers.

"Like granite mountains—the tower of Babel," Berel mused aloud.

"How do they ever walk up to the top?" asked the bewildered old mother.

"Walk!" cried Moisheh, overjoyed at the chance to hand out information. "There are elevators in America. You push a button and up you fly like on wings."

Elated with this opportunity to show off his superior knowledge, he went on: "I learned myself to sign my name in America. Stop only and I'll read for you the sign from the lamp-post," and he spelled aloud, "W-a-l-l—Wall."

"And what street is this?" asked the doctor, as we came to another corner.

Moisheh coloured with confusion, and the eyes he raised to his brother were like the eyes of a trapped deer pleading to be spared. "L-i-b———" He stopped. "Oh, *weh*!" he groaned, "the word is too long for me."

"Liberty," scorned the doctor. "You are an *Amerikaner* already and you don't know Liberty?"

His own humiliation forgot in pride of his brother's knowledge, Moisheh nodded his head humbly.

"Yeh—yeh! You a *greener* and yet you know Liberty. And I, an *Amerikaner*, is stuck by the word." He turned to me with a pride that brought tears to his eyes. "Didn't I tell you my brothers were high educated? Never mind—they won't shame me in America."

A look of adoration drank in the wonder of his beloved family. Overcome with a sense of his own unworthiness, he exclaimed, "Look only on me—a nothing and a nobody." He breathed in my ear, "And such brothers!" With a new, deeper tenderness, he pressed his mother's slight form more closely to him.

"More Bolsheviki!" scoffed a passer-by.

"Trotzky's ambassadors," sneered another.

And the ridicule was taken up by a number of jeering voices.

"Poor devils!" came from a richly dressed Hebrew, resplendent in his fur collar and a diamond stud. There was in his eyes a wistful, reminiscent look. Perhaps the sight of these immigrants brought back to him the day he himself had landed, barefoot and in rags, with nothing but his dreams of America.

The street was thronged with hurrying lunch seekers as we reached lower Broadway. I glanced at Moisheh's brothers, and I could not help noticing how different was the calm and carefree expression of their faces from the furtive, frantic acquisitive look of the men in the financial district.

But the moment we reached our block the people from the stoops and windows waved their welcome. Hanneh Breineh and all the boarders, dressed up in their best, ran to meet us.

"Home!" cried the glowing Moisheh. "*Mazel-tuff!* Good luck!" answered Hanneh Breineh.

Instantly we were surrounded by the excited neighbours whose voices of welcome rose above the familiar cries of the hucksters and pedlars that lined the street.

"Give a help!" commanded Hanneh Breineh as she seized the bundles from Moisheh's numbed arms and divided them among the boarders. Then she led the procession triumphantly into her kitchen.

The table, with a profusion of festive dishes, sang aloud its welcome.

"Rockefeller's only daughter couldn't wish herself grander eatings by her own wedding," bragged the hostess as she waved the travellers to the feast. A brass pot filled with *gefulte* fish was under the festooned chandelier. A tin platter heaped high with chopped liver and onions sent forth its inviting aroma. *Tzimmes—blintzes*—a golden-roasted goose swimming in its own fat ravished the senses. Eyes and mouths watered at sight of such luscious plenty.

"White bread!—*Ach!*—white bread!" gasped the hunger-ravaged old mother. Reaching across the table, she seized the loaf in her trembling hands. "All those starving years—all those years!" she moaned, kissing its flaky whiteness as though it were a living thing.

"Sit yourself down—*muttere!*" Hanneh Breineh soothed the old woman and helped her into the chair of honour. "White bread—even white bread is nothing in America. Even the charities—a black year on them!—even the charities give white bread to the beggars."

Moisheh, beaming with joy of his loved ones' nearness, was so busy passing and repassing the various dishes to his folks that he forgot his own meal.

"*Nu*—ain't it time for you also to sit yourself down like a person?" urged Hanneh Breineh.

"*Tekeh—tekeh!*" added his mother. "Take something to your mouth."

Thereupon Moisheh rolled up his sleeves and with the zest of a hungry caveman attacked the leg of a goose. He no sooner finished than he bent ravenously over the meat platter, his forehead working in rhythm to his jaws.

"Excuse me," stammered Moisheh, wiping his lips with the end of his shirt-sleeve and sticking the meat on a fork.

"What's the difference how you eat so long you got what to eat?" broke in Zaretsky, grabbing the breast of the goose and holding it to his thick lips.

His sensibilities recoiling at this cannibalistic devouring of food, Berel rose and walked to the air-shaft window. His arms shot out as though to break down the darkening wall which blotted out the daylight from the little room. "Plenty of food for the body, but no light for the soul," he murmured, not intending to be heard.

Feivel, the doctor, lit a cigarette and walked up and down the room restlessly. He stopped and faced his younger brother with a cynical smile. "I guess America is like the rest of the world—you get what you take—sunlight as well as other things——"

"How take sunlight? What do you mean?"

"I mean America is like a dish of cheese *blintzes* at a poor house. The beggars who are the head of the table and get their hands in first, they live and laugh——"

Hanneh Breineh wiped her lips with the corner of her apron and faced him indignantly. "You ain't yet finished with your first meal in America and already you're blowing from yourself like it's coming to you yet better."

"But why come to America?" defended Berel, the poet, "unless it gives you what's lacking in other lands? Even in the darkest days in Russia the peasants had light and air."

"Hey, Mr. Greenhorn Doctor—and you, young feller," broke in Zaretsky, the block politician, "if you don't like it here, then the President from

America will give you a free ride back on the same ship on which you came from."

Silenced by Zaretsky's biting retort, the doctor lit a cigarette and sent leisurely clouds of smoke ceilingward.

Moisheh, who had been too absorbed in his food to follow the talk, suddenly looked up from his plate. Though unable to grasp the trend of the conversation, he intuitively sensed the hostile feeling in the room.

"Why so much high language," he asked, "when there's yet the nuts and raisins and the almonds to eat?"

A few months later Hanneh Breineh came into my room while peeling potatoes in her apron. "Greenhorns ain't what greenhorns used to be," she said, as she sat down on the edge of my cot. "Once when greenhorns came, a bone from a herring, a slice from an onion, was to them milk and honey; and now pour golden chicken fat into their necks, and they turn up their nose like it's coming to them yet better."

"What is it now?" I laughed.

Hanneh Breineh rose. "Listen only to what is going on," she whispered, as she noiselessly pushed open the door and winked to me to come over and hear.

"I'm yet in debt over my neck. In God's name, how could you spend out so much money for only a little pleasure," remonstrated Moisheh.

"Do you think I'm a *schnorrer* like you? I'm a man, and I have to live," retorted the doctor.

"But two dollars for one evening in the opera only, when for ten cents you could have seen the grandest show in the movies!"

The doctor's contemptuous glance softened into a look of condescending pity. "After all, my presser of pants, what a waste the opera would be on you. Your America is the movies."

"Two dollars!" cried the little old mother, wringing her hands despairingly. "Moisheh didn't yet pay out for the ship tickets."

"Ship tickets—bah!—I wish he had never brought us to this golden country—dirt, darkness, houses like stalls for cattle!" And in a fury of disgust, not unmitigated with shame at his loss of temper, he slammed the door behind him.

"*Oi weh!*" wailed the careworn old mother. "Two dollars for an opera, and in such bad times!"

"*Ach! Mammeniu*," Moisheh defended, "maybe Feivel ain't like us. Remember he's high-educated. He needs the opera like I need the bite of bread. Maybe even more yet. I can live through without even the bite of bread, but Feivel must have what wills itself in him."

Hanneh Breineh closed the door and turned to me accusingly. "What's the use from all your education, if that's what kind of people it makes?"

"Yes," I agreed with Hanneh Breineh. "Education without heart is a curse."

Hanneh Breineh bristled. "I wish I should only be cursed with an education. It's only by the Americans education is nothing. It used to be an honour in Russia to shine a doctor's shoes for him."

"So you're for education, after all?" I ventured, trying the impossible—to pin Hanneh Breineh down.

"Bloodsuckers!" Hanneh Breineh hissed. "Moisheh dries out the marrow from his head worrying for the dollar, and these high-educated brothers sit themselves on top of his neck like leeches. Greenhorns—opera—the world is coming to an end!"

Work with the Immigration Department took me to Washington for almost a year. As soon as I returned to New York I went to the only home I knew—Hanneh Breineh's lodging-house.

My old friend, Moisheh, greeted me at the door. "*Teacherin!*" he cried, with a shout of welcome, and then called to his mother. "Come quick. See only who is here!"

Sleeves rolled up and hands full of dough, the little soul hurried in. "The sky is falling to the earth!" she cried. "You here? And are you going to stay?"

"Sure will she stay," said Moisheh, helping me remove my things.

"And where are Hanneh Breineh and the boarders?" I questioned.

"Out on a picnic by Coney Island."

"And why didn't you and your mother go?"

"I got to cook Feivel's dinner," she gesticulated with doughy palms.

"And I got my Coney Island here," said Moisheh.

To my great delight I saw he had been reading the life of Lincoln—the book I had left him the day I went away.

"My head is on fire thinking and dreaming from Lincoln. It shines before my face so real, I feel myself almost talking to him."

Moisheh's eyes were alive with light, and as I looked at him I felt for the first time a strange psychic resemblance between Moisheh and Lincoln. Could it be that the love for his hero had so transformed him as to make him almost resemble him?

"Lincoln started life as a nothing and a nobody," Moisheh went on, dreamily, "and he made himself for the President from America—maybe there's yet a chance for me to make something from myself?"

"Sure there is. Show only what's in you and all America reaches out to help you."

"I used to think that I'd die a presser by pants. But since I read from Lincoln, something happened in me. I feel I got something for America—only I don't know how to give it out. I'm yet too much of a dummox——"

"What's in us must come out. I feel America needs you and me as much as she needs her Rockefellers and Morgans. Rockefellers and Morgans only pile up mountains of money; we bring to America the dreams and desires of ages—the youth that never had a chance to be young—the choked lives that never had a chance to live."

A shadow filmed Moisheh's brooding eyes. "I can't begin yet to think from myself for a few years. First comes my brothers. If only Feivel would work for himself up for a big doctor and Berel for a big writer then I'll feel myself free to do something...."

"Shah! I got great news for you," Moisheh announced. "Feivel has already his doctor's office."

"Where did he get all the money?"

"On the instalment plan I got him the chair and the office things. Now he's beginning to earn already enough to pay almost half his rent."

"Soon he'll be for dinner." The old lady jumped up. "I got to get his eating ready before he comes." And she hastened back to the kitchen stove.

"And Berel—what does he do?" I inquired.

"Berel ain't working yet. He's still writing from his head," explained Moisheh. "Wait only and I'll call him. He's locked himself up in his bedroom; nobody should bother him."

"Berel!" he called, tapping respectfully at the door.

"*Yuk!*" came in a voice of nervous irritation. "What is it?"

"The *teacherin* is here," replied Moisheh.

"Only a minute."

"It's me," I added. "I'd like to see you."

Berel came out, hair dishevelled, with dreamy, absent look, holding pencil and paper in his hand. "I was just finishing a poem," he said in greeting to me.

"I have been looking for your name in the magazines. Have you published anything yet?"

"I—publish in the American magazines?" he flung, hurt beyond words. "I wouldn't mix my art with their empty drivel."

"But, surely, there are some better magazines," I protested.

"Pshah! Their best magazines—the pink-and-white jingles that they call poetry are not worth the paper they're printed on. America don't want poets. She wants plumbers."

"But what will you do with the poetry you write?"

"I'll publish it myself. Art should be free, like sunlight and beauty. The only compensation for the artist is the chance to feed hungry hearts. If only Moisheh could give me the hundred dollars I'd have my volume printed at once."

"But how can I raise all that money when I'm not yet paid out with Feivel's doctor's office?" remonstrated Moisheh. "Don't you think if—maybe you'd get a little job?"

An expression of abstraction came over Betel's face, and he snapped, impatiently: "Yes—yes—I told you that I would look for a job. But I must write this while I have the inspiration."

"Can't you write your inspiration out in the evening?" faltered Moisheh. "If you could only bring in a few dollars a week to help pay ourselves out to the instalment man."

Berel looked at his brother with compassionate tolerance. "What are to you the things of the soul? All you care for is money—money—money! You'd want me to sell my soul, my poetry, my creative fire—to hand you a few dirty dollars."

The postman's whistle and the cry, "Berel Cinski!"

Moisheh hurried downstairs and brought back a large return envelope.

"Another one of those letters back," deplored the mother, untactfully. "You're only for making the post office rich with the stamps from Moisheh's blood money."

"Dammit!" Defeat enraged the young poet to the point of brutality. "Stop nagging me and mixing in with things you don't understand!" He struck the rude table with his clenched fist. "It's impossible to live with you thickheads—numskulls—money-grubbing worms."

He threw on his hat and coat and paused for a moment glowering in the doorway. "Moisheh," he demanded, "give me a quarter for car fare. I have to go uptown to the library." Silently the big brother handed him the money, and Berel flung himself out of the room.

The door had no sooner closed on the poet than the doctor sauntered into the room. After a hasty "Hallo!" he turned to Moisheh. "I've had a wonderful opportunity offered me—but I can't take advantage of it."

"What!" cried Moisheh, his face brightening.

"My landlord invited me to his house to-night, to meet his only daughter."

"Why not go?" demanded Moisheh.

"Sure you got to go," urged the mother, as she placed the food before him. "The landlord only got to see how smart you are and he'll pull you in the richest customers from uptown."

Feivel looked at his clothes with resigned contempt. "H—m," he smiled bitterly. "Go in this shabby suit? I have too much respect for myself."

There was troubled silence. Both brother and mother were miserable that their dear one should be so deprived.

Moisheh moved over to the window, a worried look on his face. Presently he turned to his brother. "I'd give you the blood from under my nails for you but I'm yet so behind with the instalment man."

The doctor stamped his foot impatiently. "I simply have to have a suit! It's a question of life and death.... Think of the chance! The landlord took a liking to me—rich as Rockefeller—and an only daughter. If he gives me a start in an uptown office I could *coin* money. All I need is a chance—the right location. Ten—twenty—fifty dollars an hour. There's no limit to a dentist's fee. If he sets me up on Riverside Drive I could charge a hundred dollars for work I get five for in Rutgers Street!"

"Can I tear myself in pieces? Squeeze the money from my flesh?"

"But do you realize that, once I get uptown, I could earn more in an hour than you could in a month? I'll pay you back every penny a hundred times over."

"*Nu*—tell me only—what can I do? Anything you'll say———"

"Why—you have your gold watch."

Moisheh's hand leaped to the watch in his vest pocket. "My gold watch! My prize from the night school?" he pleaded. "It ain't just a watch—it's given me by the principal for never being absent for a whole year."

"Oh, rot!—you, with your sentimentality! Try to understand something once." The doctor waved his objections aside. "Once I get my start in an uptown office I can buy you a dozen watches. I'm telling you my whole future depends on the front I put up at the landlord's house, and still you hesitate!"

Moisheh looked at his watch, fingering it. His eyes filled with tears. "*Oi weh!*" he groaned. "It's like a piece from my heart. My prize from the night school," he mumbled, brokenly; "but take it if you got to have it."

"You'll get it back," confidently promised the doctor, "get it back a hundred times over." And as he slipped the watch into his pocket, Moisheh's eyes followed it doggedly. "So long, *mammeniu*; no dinner for me to-day." Feivel bestowed a hasty good-bye caress upon his old mother.

———

The doctor was now living in an uptown boarding-house, having moved some weeks before, giving the excuse that for his business it was necessary to cultivate an uptown acquaintance. But he still kept up his office in Rutgers Street.

One morning after he had finished treating my teeth, he took up a cigarette, nervously lit it, attempted to smoke, and then threw it away. I had never seen the suave, complacent man so unnerved and fidgety. Abruptly he stopped in front of me and smiled almost affectionately.

"You are the very person I want to speak to this morning—you are the only person I want to speak to," he repeated.

I was a little startled, for his manner was most unlike him. Seldom did he even notice me, just as he did not notice most of Moisheh's friends. But his exuberant joyousness called out my instinctive response, and before I knew it I was saying, "If there's anything I can do for you I'll be only too happy."

He took a bill from his pocket, placed it in my hand, and said, with repressed excitement: "I want you to take my mother and Moisheh to see 'Welcome Stranger.' It's a great show. It's going to be a big night with me, and I want them to be happy, too."

I must have looked puzzled, for he narrowed his eyes and studied me, twice starting to speak, and both times stopping himself.

"You must have thought me a selfish brute all this time," he began. "But I've only been biding my time. I must make the most of myself, and now is my only chance—to rise in the world."

He stopped again, paced the floor several times, placed a chair before me, and said: "Please sit down. I want to talk to you."

There was a wistful pleading in his voice that none could resist, and for the first time I was aware of the compelling humanness of this arrogant intellectual.

"I'll tell you everything just as it is," he started. And then he stopped again. "*Ach!*" he groaned. "There's something I would like to talk over with you—but I just can't. You wouldn't understand.... A great thing is happening in my life to-night—but I can't confide it to anyone—none can understand. But—I ask of you just this: will you give Moisheh and my mother a good time? Let the poor devils enjoy themselves for once?"

As I walked out of the office, the bill still crumpled in my hand, I reproached myself for my former harsh condemnation of the doctor. Perhaps all those months, when I had thought him so brutally selfish, he had been building for the future.

But what was this mysterious good fortune that he could not confide to anyone—and that none could understand?

"Doctor Feivel gave me money to take you to the theatre," I announced as I entered the house.

"Theatre!" chorused Moisheh and his mother, excitedly.

"Yes," I said. "Feivel seemed so happy to-day, and he wanted you to share his happiness."

"Feivel, the golden heart!" The old mother's eyes were misty with emotion.

"*Ach!* Didn't I tell you even if my brother is high-educated, he won't shame himself from us?" Moisheh faced me triumphantly. "I was so afraid since he moved himself into an uptown boarding-house that maybe we are losing him, even though he still kept up his office on Rutgers Street." Moisheh's eyes shone with delight.

"I'll tell you a little secret," said he, leaning forward confidentially. "I'm planning to give a surprise to Feivel. In another month I'll pay myself out for the last of Feivel's office things. And for days and nights I'm going around thinking and dreaming about buying him an electric sign. Already I made the price with the instalment man for it." By this time his recital was ecstatic. "And think only—what *mein* doctor will say, when he'll come one morning from his uptown boarding-house and find my grand surprise waiting for him over his office door!"

All the way to the theatre Moisheh and his mother drank in the glamour and the glitter of the electric signs of Broadway.

"*Gottuniu!* If I only had the money for such a sign for Feivel," Moisheh sighed, pointing to the chewing-gum advertisement on the roof of a building near the Astor. "If I only had Rockefeller's money, I'd light up America with Feivel's doctor sign!"

When we reached the theatre, we found we had come almost an hour too early.

"Never mind—*mammeniu!*" Moisheh took his mother's arm tenderly. "We'll have time now to walk ourselves along and see the riches and lights from America."

"I should live so," he said, surveying his mother affectionately. "That red velvet waist and this new shawl over your head makes your face so shine, everybody stops to give a look on you."

"Yeh—yeh! You're always saying love words to every woman you see."

"But this time it's my mother, so I mean it from my heart."

Moisheh nudged me confidentially. "*Teacherin!* See only how a little holiday lifts up my *mammeniu*! Don't it dance from her eyes the joy like from a young girl?"

"Stop already making fun from your old mother."

"You old?" Moisheh put his strong arm around his mother's waist. "Why, people think we're a young couple on our honeymoon."

"Honeymoon—*ach!*" The faded face shone with inward visioning. "My only wish is to see for my eyes my sons marry themselves in good luck. What's my life—but only the little hope from my children? To dance with the bride on my son's wedding will make me the happiest mother from America."

"Feivel will soon give you that happiness," responded Moisheh. "You know how the richest American-born girls are trying to catch on to him. And no matter how grand the girl he'll marry himself to, you'll have the first place of honour by the wedding."

As we turned in at Forty-fifth Street a curious crowd blocked our path. A row of sleek limousines stood before the arched entrance of the Van Suydden Hotel.

"Look only—a wedding! Let's give a look on the bride!" exclaimed Moisheh's mother, eagerly. A wedding was, in her religion, the most significant ceremony in life. And for her sake we elbowed our way towards the front.

A procession of bridesmaids in shimmering chiffons, bedecked with flowers, were the first to tread the carpeted steps.

Then we saw the bride.... And then——Good God!—was it possible?

Moisheh clutched his mother's hand convulsively. Could it really be their Feivel?

The two stood gaping blindly, paralysed by the scene before them.

Suddenly—roused by the terrible betrayal—the mother uttered a distorted sob of grief. "Feivel—son *mein*! What have you done to me?"

Moisheh grasped the old woman more firmly as the bride tossed her head coquettishly and turned possessive eyes on her husband—their son and brother.

The onlookers murmured appreciatively, thrilled by the pretty romance.

Enraged by the stupid joy of the crowd which mocked her misery, the old mother broke from Moisheh's hold with wiry strength and clawed wildly at the people around her.

"Feivel—black curses——!" she hissed—and then she crumpled, fainting, into Moisheh's arms.

Unaware of the disturbance outside, the happy couple passed into the festive reception hall.

With quick self-control, Moisheh motioned to a taxicab out of which had just emerged another wedding guest. Then he gently lifted the fainting form of the little mother in beside him.

And all through the night the bitter tears of betrayed motherhood poured over the shrunken bosom where Feivel, as a suckling infant, had once helped himself to life.

TO THE STARS

§ 1

"There are too many writers and too few cooks." The dean laughed at her outright. His superior glance placed her. "The trouble with you is that you are a Russian Jewess. You want the impossible."

Sophie Sapinsky's mouth quivered at the corners, and her teeth bit into the lower lip to still its trembling.

"How can you tell what's possible in me before I had a chance?" she said.

"My dear child"—Dean Lawrence tried to be kind—"the magazine world is overcrowded with native-born writers who do not earn their salt. What chance is there for you, with your immigrant English? You could never get rid of your foreign idiom. Quite frankly, I think you are too old to begin."

"I'm not so old like I look." Sophie heard a voice that seemed to come from somewhere within her speak for her. "I'm only old from the crushed-in things that burn me up. It dies in me, my heart, if I don't give out what's in me."

"My dear young woman"—the dean's broad tolerance broke forth into another laugh—"you are only one of the many who think that they have something to say that the world is languishing to hear." His easy facetiousness stung her into further vehemence.

"But I'm telling you I ain't everybody." With her fist she struck his desk, oblivious of what she was doing. "I'm smart from myself, not from books. I never had a chance when I was young, so I got to *make my chance* when I'm 'too old.' I feel I could yet be younger than youth if I could only catch on to the work I love."

"Take my advice. Retain the position that assures you a living. Apply yourself earnestly to it, and you will secure a measure of satisfaction."

The dean turned to the mahogany clock on his desk. Sophie Sapinsky was quick to take the hint. She had taken up too much of his time, but she could not give up without another effort.

"I can't make good at work that chokes me."

"Well, then see the head of the English department," he said, with a gesture of dismissal.

The professor of English greeted Sophie with a tired, lifeless smile that fell like ashes on her heart. A chill went through her as she looked at his bloodless face. But the courage of despair drove her to speak.

"I wasted all my youth slaving for bread, but now I got to do what I want to do. For me—oh, you can't understand—but for me, it's a case of life or death. I got to be a writer, and I want to take every course in English and literature from the beginning to the end."

The professor did not laugh at Sophie Sapinsky as the dean had done. He had no life left for laughter. But his cold scrutiny condemned her.

"I know," she pleaded, "I ain't up to those who had a chance to learn from school, but inside me I'm always thinking from life, just like Emerson. I understand Emerson like he was my own brother. And he says: 'Trust yourself. Hold on to the thoughts that fly through your head, and the world has got to listen to you even if you're a nobody.' Ideas I got plenty. What I want to learn from the college is only the words, the quick language to give out what thinks itself in me—just like Emerson."

The preposterous assumption of this ignorant immigrant girl in likening herself to the revered sage of Concord staggered the professor. He coughed.

"Well—er"—he paused to get the exact phrase to set her right—"Emerson, in his philosophy, assumed a tolerant attitude that, unfortunately, the world does not emulate. Perhaps you remember the unhappy outcome of your English entrance examination."

Sophie Sapinsky reddened painfully. The wound of her failure was still fresh.

"In order to be eligible for our regular college courses, you would have to spend two or three years in preparation."

Blindly, Sophie turned to go. She reached for the door. The professor's perfunctory good-bye fell on deaf ears.

She swung the door open. The president of the college stood before her. She remembered it was he who had welcomed the extension students on the evening of her first attendance. He moved deferentially aside for her to pass. For one swift instant Sophie looked into kindly eyes. "Could he understand? Should I cry out to him to help me?" flashed through her mind. But before she could say a word he passed and the door had closed.

Sophie stopped in the hall. Had she the courage to wait until he came out? "He's got feelings," her instincts urged her. "He's not an *all-rightnik*, a stone heart like the rest of them."

"*Ach!*" cried her shattered spirit, "what would he, the head of them all, have to do with me? He wouldn't even want to stop to listen."

Too crushed to endure another rebuff, she dragged her leaden feet down the stairs and out into the street. All the light went out of her eyes, the strength out of her arms and fingers. She could think or feel nothing but the choked sense of her defeat.

That night she lay awake staring into the darkness. Every nerve within her cried aloud with the gnawing ache of her unlived life. Out of the dim corners the spectre of her stunted girlhood rose to mock her—the wasted, poverty-stricken years smothered in the steaming pots of other people's kitchens. "Must I always remain buried alive in the black prison of my dumbness? Can't I never learn to give out what's in me? Must I choke myself in the smoke of my own fire?"

Centuries of suppression, generations of illiterates, clamoured in her: "Show them what's in you! If you can't write in college English, write in 'immigrant English.'"

She flung from her the college catalogue. About to trample on it, she stopped. The catalogue had fallen open at the photograph of the president. There looked up at her the one kind face in that heartless college world. The president's eyes gazed once more steadily into hers. Sophie hesitated; but not to be thwarted of her vengeance, she tore out his picture and laid it on the table, then she ripped the catalogue, and stuffed the crumpled pages into the stove. It roared up the chimney like the song of the Valkyrie. She threw back her head with triumph, and once more her eyes met the president's.

"Let them burn, these dead-heads. Who are they, the bosses of education? What are they that got the say over me if I'm fit to learn or not fit to learn? Dust and ashes, ashes and dust. But you," she picked up the picture, "you still got some life. But if you got life, don't their dry dust choke you?"

The wrestlings of her sleepless night only strengthened her resolve to do the impossible, just because it seemed impossible. "I can't tear the stars out of heaven if it wills itself in me," her youth cried in her. "Whether I know how to write or don't know how to write, I'll be a writer."

§ 2

She was at the steaming stove of the restaurant at the usual hour the next morning. She stewed the same *tzimmas*, fried the same *blintzee*, stuffed the same *miltz*. But she was no longer the same. Her head was in a whirl with golden dreams of her visionary future.

All at once a scream rent the air.

"*Koosh!* where in goodness' name is your head?" thundered her employer. "The *blintzee* burning in front of her nose, and she stands there like a *yok* with her eyes in the air!"

"Excuse me," she mumbled in confusion, setting down the pan. "I was only thinking for a minute."

"Thinking!" His greasy face purpled with rage. "Do I pay you to think or to cook? For what do I give you such wages? What's the world coming to? *Pfui!* A cook, a greenhorn, a nothing—also me a thinker!"

Sophie's eyes flamed.

"Maybe in Smyrna, from where you come, a cook is a nothing. In America everybody is a person."

"Bolshevik!" he yelled. "Look only what fresh mouths the unions make from them! Y'understand me, in my restaurant one thing on a time: you cook or you think. If you wan' to think, you'll think outside."

"All right, then; give me my wages!" she retorted, flaring up. "The Tsar is dead. In America cooks are also people."

Sophie tore off her apron, and thrust it at the man.

To the cheapest part of the East Side she went in her search for a room. Through the back alleys and yards she sought for a place that promised to be within her means. And then a smeared square of cardboard held between the iron grating of a basement window caught her eye. "Room to let—a bargain—cheap!"

"Only three dollars a month," said the woman in answer to Sophie's inquiry.

The girl opened a grimy window that faced a blank wall.

"*Oi, weh!* not a bit of air!"

"What do you need yet air for the winter?" cried Hanneh Breineh. "When the cold comes, the less air that blows into your room, the warmer you can keep yourself. And when it gets hot in summer you can take your mattress up on the roof. Everybody sleeps on the roof in summer."

"But there's so little light," said Sophie.

"What more light do you yet need? A room is only for to sleep by night. When you come home from work, it's dark, anyway. *Gottuniu!* it's so dark on my heart with trouble, what difference does it make a little darkness in the room?"

"But I have to work in my room all day. I must have it light."

"*Nu*, I'll let you keep the gas lighted all day long," Hanneh Breineh promised.

"Three dollars a month," deliberated Sophie. The cheapness would give her a sense of freedom that would make up for the lack of light and air. She paid down her first month's rent.

Her house, securely hers. Yet with the flash of triumph came a stab of bitterness. All that was hers was so wretched and so ugly! Had her eager spirit, eager to give, no claim to a bit of beauty, a shred of comfort?

Over the potato-barrel she flung a red shawl, once her mother's, and looked through her bag for something to cover an ugly break in the plaster. She could find nothing but the page torn from the college catalogue.

"It's not so sunny and airy here as in your college office," she said, tacking the photograph on the wall; "but maybe you'd be a realer man if once in your life you had to put up with a hole like this for a room."

Sophie spread her papers on the cot beside her. With tense fingers she wrote down the title of her story, then stopped, and stared wildly at the ceiling.

Where was the vision that had haunted her all these days? Where were the thoughts and feelings that surged like torrents through her soul? Merely the act of putting her pencil to paper, her thoughts became a blur, her feelings a dumb ache in her heart.

Ach, why must she kill herself to say what can never be said in words? But how did Emerson and Shakespeare seize hold of their vision? What was the source of their deathless power?

The rusty clock struck six.

"I ought to run out now for the stale bread, or it will be all sold out, and I will have to pay twice as much for the fresh," flashed through her mind.

"*Oi weh!*" she wailed, covering her eyes, "it's a stomach slave I am, not a writer. I forget my story, I forget everything, thinking only of saving a few pennies."

She dragged herself back to the page in front of her and resumed her task with renewed vigour.

"Sarah Lubin was sixteen years old when she came to America. She came to get an education, but she had to go to a factory for bread," she wrote laboriously, and then drew back to study her work. The sentences were wooden, dead, inanimate things. The words laughed up at her, mockingly.

Perhaps she was not a writer, after all. Writers never started stories in this way. Her eyes wandered over to the bed, a hard, meagre cot. "I must remember to fix the leg, or it will tip to-night," she mused.

"Here I am," she cried despairingly, "thinking of my comforts again! And I thought I'd want nothing; I'd live only to write." Her head sank to the rough edge of the potato-barrel. "Perhaps I was a fool to give up all for this writing."

"Too many writers and too few cooks": the dean's words closed like a noose around her anguished soul.

When she looked up, the kind face of the college president smiled down at her.

"Then what is it in me that's tearing and gnawing and won't let me rest?" she pleaded. The calm faith of the eyes levelled steadily at her seemed to rebuke her despair. The sure faith of that lofty face lifted her out of herself. She was humble before such unwavering power. "*Ach!*" she prayed, "how can I be so sure like you? Help me!"

Sophie became a creature possessed. She lived for one idea, was driven by one resistless passion, to write. As the weeks and months passed and her savings began to dwindle, her cheeks grew paler and thinner, the shadows under her restless eyes were black hollows of fear.

There came a day more deadly than death, when she had to face failure. She took out the thinning wad from her stocking and counted out her remaining cash: one, two, three dollars, and some nickels and dimes. How long before the final surrender? If she kept up her rigorous ration of dry bread and oatmeal, two or three weeks more at most. And then?

An end to dreams. An end to ambition. Back to the cook-stove, back to the stifling smells of *tzimmas*, hash, and *miltz*.

No, she would never let herself sink back to the kitchen. But where could she run from the terror of starvation?

The bitterest barb of her agony was her inability to surrender. She was crushed, beaten, but she could not give up the battle. The unvoiced dream in her still clamoured and ached and strained to find voice. A resistless something in her that transcended reason rose up in defiance of defeat.

§ 3

"A black year on the landlord!" screamed Hanneh Breineh through the partition. "The rent he raised, so what does he need to worry yet if the gas freezes? *Gottuniu!* freeze should only the marrow from his bones!"

Sophie turned back to the little stove in an attempt to light the gas under the pan of oatmeal. The feeble flame flickered and with a faint protest went out. Hanneh Breineh poked in her tousled head for sympathy.

"Woe is me! Woe on the poor what ain't yet sick enough for the hospital!"

As the chill of the gathering dusk intensified, Sophie seemed to see herself carried out on a stretcher to the hospital, numb, frozen.

"God from the world! better a quick death than this slow freezing!" With the perpetual gnawing of hunger sapping her strength, Sophie had not the courage to face another night of torment. Drawing her shabby shawl more tightly around her, she hurried out. "Where now?" she asked as a wave of stinging snow blinded her. Hanneh Breineh's words came back to her: "the hospital!" Why not? Surely they couldn't refuse to shelter her just overnight in a storm like this.

But when she reached the Beth Israel her heart sank. She looked in timidly at the warm, beckoning lights.

"*Ach!* how can I have the gall to ask them to take me in? They'll think I'm only a beggar from the street."

She paced the driveway of the building, back and forth and up and down, in envy of the sick who enjoyed the luxury of warmth.

"To the earth with my healthy body!" she cursed. "Why can't I only break a bone or something?"

With a sudden courage of despair she mounted the steps to the superintendent's office; but one glance of the man's well-fed face robbed her of her nerve.

She sank down on the bench of the waiting applicants, glancing stealthily at the others, feeling all the guilt of a condemned criminal.

When her turn came, the blood in her ears pounded from terror and humiliation. She could not lift her eyes from the floor to face this feelingless judge of the sick and the suffering.

"I'm so killed with the cold," she stammered, twisting the fringes of her shawl. "If I could only warm myself up in a bed for the night——"

The man looked at her suspiciously.

"If we fill up our place with people like you, we'll have no room left for the sick. We have a 'flu epidemic."

"So much you're doing for the 'flu people, why can't you help me before I get it?" She spoke with that suppressed energy which was the keynote of her whole personality.

"Have you a fever?" he asked, his professional eye arrested by the unnatural flush on her face.

"Fever?" she mumbled. "A person has got to be already dead in his coffin before you'd lift a finger to help." She sped from the office into the dreary reception-hall.

On her way out her eye was caught by the black-faced type on the cover of a magazine that lay on the centre-table.

SHORT-STORY COMPETITION

A Five-Hundred-Dollar Prize for the Best Love-Story of a Working-Girl

As she read the magical words, the colour rushed to her cheeks. Forgotten was the humiliation of the superintendent's refusal to take her in, forgotten were the cold, the hunger. Her whole being leaped at the words:

"Write your own love-story, but if you have never lived love, let it be your dream of love."

"Your dream of love." The words were as wine in her blood. Was there ever a girl who hungered and dreamed of love as she? It was as though in the depths of her poverty and want the fates had challenged her to give substance to her dreams. She stumbled out of the huge building, her feet in the snow, her mind in the clouds.

"God from the world! the gas is burning again!" cried Hanneh Breineh as she groped her way back into her cellar-room. "The children are dancing over the fire like for a holiday. All day they had nothing to warm in their bellies, and the coffee tastes like wine from heaven."

"Wine from heaven!" repeated the girl. "What wine but love from heaven?" and she clutched the magazine more tightly to her shrunken chest.

In the flicker of the gas-jet the photograph on the wall greeted her like a living thing. With the feel of the steady gaze upon her, she re-read the message that was to her an invitation and a challenge; and as she read, the dingy little room became alive with light. The understanding eyes seemed to pour vision into her soul. What was the purpose of all the harsh experiences that had been hers till now but to make her see just this, that love, and love only, was the one vital force of life? What was the purpose of all the privation and want she had endured but to make her see more poignantly this ethereal essence of love? The walls of her little room dissolved. The longing for love that lay dumb within her all her years took shape in human form. More real than life, closer than the beat within her heart, was this radiant, all-consuming vision that possessed her.

She groped for pencil and paper and wrote, unaware that she was writing. It was as though a hand stronger than her own was laid upon hers. Her power seemed to come from some vast, fathomless source. The starved passions of all the starved ages poured through her in rhythmic torrent of words—words that flashed and leaped with the resistless fire of youth burning through generations of suppression.

Not until daylight filtered through the grating of her window did the writing cease, nor was she aware of any fatigue. An ethereal lightness, a sense of having escaped from the trammels of her body, lifted her as on wings. Her radiant face met the responsive glow of understanding that shone down on her from the wall. "It's your light shining through me," she exulted. "It's your kind eyes looking into mine that made my dumbness speak."

For the moment the contest was forgotten. She was seized by an irresistible impulse to take her outpourings to the man who had inspired her. "Let him only see what music he made of me." Gathering tightly to her heart the scribbled sheets of paper, she hurried to the university.

A whole hour she waited at his office door. As she saw him coming, she could wait no longer, but ran towards him.

"Read it only," she said, thrusting the manuscript at the bewildered man. "I'll be back in an hour."

"What exotic creature was this, with her scattered pages of scrawling script and eager eyes?" President Irvine wondered. He concluded she was one of the immigrant group before which he had lectured.

§ 4

She returned, to find the manuscript still in his hand.

"Tell me," he asked with an enthusiasm new to him, "where did you get all this?"

"From the hunger in me. I was born to beat out the meaning of things out of my own heart."

Puzzled, he studied her. She was thin, gaunt, with a wasting power of frustrated passion in young flesh. There was the shadow of blank nights staring out of her eyes. Here was a personality, he thought, who might reveal to him those intangible qualities of the immigrant—qualities he could not grasp, which baffled, fascinated him.

He questioned her, and she poured out her story to him with eager abandon.

"I couldn't be an actress or a singer, because you got to be young and pretty for that; but for a writer nobody cares who or what you are so long as the thoughts you give out are beautiful."

He laughed, and it was an appreciative, genial laugh.

"You ain't at all like a professor, cold and hard like ice. You are a person so real," she naïvely said, interrupting the tale of her early struggles, her ambitions, and the repulse that had been hers in this very university of his. And then in sudden apprehension she cried out: "Maybe the dean and the English professor were right. Maybe only those with a long education get a hearing in America. If you would only fix this up for me—change the immigrant English."

"Fix it up?" he protested. "There are things in life bigger than rules of grammar. The thing that makes art live and stand out throughout the ages is sincerity. Unfortunately, education robs many of us of the power to give spontaneously, as mother earth gives, as the child gives.

"You have poured out not a part, but the whole of yourself. That's why it can't be measured by any of the prescribed standards. It's uniquely you."

Her face lighted with joy at his understanding.

"I never knew why I hated to be Americanized. I was always burning to dig out the thoughts from my own mind."

"Yes, your power lies in that you are yourself. Your message is that of your people, and it is all the stronger because you are not a so-called assimilated immigrant."

Ach! just to hear him talk! It was like the realization of a power in life itself to hold her up and carry her to the heights.

"Will you leave this manuscript here, so I can have my secretary type it for you?" he asked as he took her to the door. "I can have it done easily. And I shall write you when I'll have time for another long talk about your work."

Only after she had left did she fully realize the wonder of this man's kindness.

"That's America," she whispered. "Where but in America could something so beautiful happen? A crazy, choked-in thing like me and him such a gentleman talking together about art and life like born equals. I poverty, and he plenty; I ignorance, and he knowledge; I from the bottom, and he from the top, and yet he making me feel like we were from always friends."

A few days later the promised note came. How quick he was with his help, as if she were his only concern! Bare-headed, uncoated, she ran to him, this prince of kindness, repeating over and over again the words of the letter.

Her spirit crashed to the ground when she learned that he had been suddenly called to a conference at Washington. "He would return in a fortnight," said the model-mannered secretary who answered her feverish questions.

Wait a fortnight? She couldn't. Why, the contest would be over by that time. Then it struck her, the next best thing—the professor of English. With a typewritten manuscript in her hand, he must listen to her. And just to be admitted to his short-story class for one criticism was all she would ask.

But small a favour as it seemed to her, it was greater than the professor was in a position to grant.

"To concede to your request would establish a precedent that would be at variance with the university regulations," he vouchsafed.

"University regulations, precedents? What are you talking?" And clutching at his sleeve, hysterically, she pleaded: "Just this once, my life hangs on getting this story perfect, and you can save me by this one criticism."

Her burning desire knew no barrier, recognized no higher authority. And the professor, contrary to his reason, contrary to his experienced judgment, yielded without knowing why to the preposterous demands of this immigrant girl.

In the end of the last row of the lecture-hall Sophie waited breathlessly for the professor to get to her story. After a lifetime of waiting it came. As from a great distance she heard him announce the title.

"This was not written by a member of the class," he went on, "but is the attempt of a very ambitious young person. Its lack of form demonstrates the importance of the fundamentals of technique in which we have drilled."

His reading aloud of the manuscript was followed by a chorus of criticism— criticism that echoed the professor's own sentiments: "It's not a story; it has no plot"; "feeling without form"; "erotic, over-emotional."

She could hardly wait for the hour to be over to get back this living thing of hers that they were killing. When she left the class all the air seemed to have gone out of her lungs. She dragged her leaden feet back to her room and sank on her cot a heap of despair.

All at once she jumped up.

"What do they know, they, with only their book-learning?" If the president had understood her story, there might be others who would understand. She must have faith enough in herself to send it forth for a judgment of a world free from rules of grammar. In a fury of defiance she mailed the story.

§ 5

Weeks of tortuous waiting for news of the contest followed—weeks when she dogged the postman's footsteps and paced the lonely streets in restless suspense. How could she ever have hoped to win the prize? Why was she so starving for the golden hills on the sky? If only for one day she could stop wasting her heart for the impossible!

Exhausted, spent, she lay on her cot when Hanneh Breineh, more than usually disturbed by the girl's driven look, opened the door softly.

"Here you got it, a letter. I hope it's such good luck in it as the paper is fine."

"What's the matter?" cried Hanneh Breineh in alarm at the girl's sudden pallor as the empty envelope fluttered from limp fingers.

For answer Sophie held up the cheque.

"Five hundred dollars," she cried, "and the winner of the first prize!"

Hanneh Breineh felt the cheque. She read it. It was actually true. Five hundred dollars! In a flurry of excitement she called the neighbours in the hall-ways, and then hurried to the butcher, pushing through the babbling women who crowded around the counter. "People listen only! My *roomerkeh* got a five-hundred-dollar prize!"

"Five hundred dollars?" The words leaped from lips to lips like fire in the air. "*Ach!* only the little bit of luck! Did she win it on the lotteree?"

"Not from the lottery. Just wrote something from her head. And you ought to see her, only a dried-up bone of a girl, and yet so smart."

In a few moments Sophie was mobbed in her cellar by the gesticulating crowd of women who hurried in to gaze upon the miracle of good luck. With breathless awe hands felt her, and, reverently, the cheque. Yes, even mouths watered with an envy that was almost worship. They fell on her neck and kissed her.

"May we all live to have such luck to get rich quick!" they chorused.

The following day Sophie's picture was in the Jewish evening paper. The Ghetto was drunk with pride because one of their number, and "only a dried-up bone of a girl," had written a story good enough to be printed in a magazine of America. Their dreams of romance had found expression in the overwhelming success of this greenhorn cook.

In one day Sophie was elevated to a position of social importance by her achievement. When she walked in the street, people pointed at her with their fingers. She was deluged with requests "to give a taste" of the neighbours' cooking.

When she went to the baker for her usual stale bread, the man picked out the finest loaf.

"Fresh bread for you in honour of your good luck. And here's yet an apple *strudel* for good measure." Nor would he take the money she offered. "Only eat it with good health. I'm paid enough with the honour that somebody with such luck steps into my store."

"Of course," explained Hanneh Breineh. "People will give you the last bite from their mouth when you're lucky, because you don't need their favours. But if you're poor, they're afraid to be good to you, so you should not hang on their necks for help."

But the greatest surprise that awaited Sophie was the letter from the professor congratulating her upon her success.

"The students have unanimously voted you to be their guest of honour at luncheon on Saturday," it read. "May we hope for the honour of your company on that occasion?"

The sky is falling to the earth—she a guest of honour of a well-fed, well-dressed world! She to break bread with those high up in rules of grammar! Sophie laughed aloud for the first time in months. Lunch at the hotel! A vision of snowy tablecloths, silver forks, delicate china, and sparkling glasses dazzled her. Yes, she would go, and go as she was. The clothes that had been good enough to starve and struggle in must be good enough to be feasted and congratulated in.

She was surprised at the sense of cold detachment with which she entered the hotel lobby.

"Maybe it's my excuse to myself for going that makes me feel that I'm so above it," she told herself. The grandeur, the lights, the lustre, and glamour of the magnificent hotel—she took it all in, her nose in the air.

At the entrance of the banquet-hall stood the professor, smiling, smiling. And all these people in silks and furs and broadcloth wanted to shake hands with her. Again, without knowing why, she longed to laugh aloud.

Not until Professor ——, smiling more graciously than ever, reached the close of his speech, not until he referred to her for the third time as having reached "the stars through difficulties," did she realize that she who had looked on, she who had listened, she who had wanted so to laugh, was a person quite different from the uncouth girl with the shabby sweater and broken shoes whom the higher-ups were toasting and flattering.

"I've never made a talk yet in my life," she said in answer to the calls for "Speech! speech!" "But these are grand words from the professor, 'to the stars through difficulties.'" She looked around on these stars of the college world whom, after all her struggles, she had reached. "Yes, 'to the stars through difficulties.'" She nodded with a queer little smile, and sat down amidst a shower of applause.

§ 6

In a daze Sophie left the heated banquet-hall. She walked blindly, struggling to get hold of herself, struggling in vain. Every reality, every human stay, seemed to slip from her. A stifled sense of emptiness weighed her down like a dead weight.

"What's the matter with me?" she cried. "Why do the higher-ups crush me so with nothing? Why is their smiling politeness only a hidden hurt in my heart?"

The flattering voices, the puppet-like smiles, the congratulations that sounded like mockery, were now so distant, so unreal as was the girl with her nose in the air. What cared these people wrapped in furs that the winter wind pierced through her shabby sweater? What cared they if her heart died in her from loneliness?

An aching need for human fellowship pressed upon her, a need for someone who cared for her regardless of failure or success. In a sudden dimming of vision she saw the only real look of sympathy that had ever warmed her soul. Of them all, this man with the understanding eyes had known that what she wanted to say was worth saying before it got into print. If she could only see him—him himself!

If she could only pass the building where he was she would feel calm and serene again! All her bitterness and resentment would dissolve, all her doubts turn to faith. Who knows? Perhaps he had come back already. Her feet seemed winged as they flew without her will, almost without her consciousness, towards the place where she thought he might be.

As she ran up the steps she knew he was there without being told. Even as she sent her name in, the door opened, and he stood there, the living light of the late afternoon glow.

He wasn't a bit startled by her sudden appearance. He merely greeted her, and led her in silence to his inner study. But there was a quality about the silence that made her feel at ease, as though he had been expecting her.

"I have things to say to you," she faltered. "Do you have time?"

For answer he pushed closer to the blazing logs an easy chair, and motioned her into it.

There no longer seemed any need to say what she had planned. His mere presence filled her with a healing peace.

"And it was so black for my eyes only a while before!" She spoke aloud her thought and paused, embarrassed.

"Black for your eyes?" he repeated, leaning towards her with an inviting interest.

"You know I was first on the table by the hotel?"

His eyebrows lifted whimsically.

"Tell me about it," he urged.

"All those higher-ups what didn't care a pinch of salt for me myself making such a fuss over a little accident of good luck!"

"Accident! You have won your way inch by inch grappling with life." His calm, compelling look seemed to flood her with strength. "You have what our colleges cannot give, the courage to face yourself, the power to think. And now all your past experiences are so much capital to be utilized. Do you see the turning-point I mean?"

"The turning-point in my life is to know I got a friend. I owe it to the world to do something, to be something, after this miracle of your kindness." And at his deepening smile, "But you are not kind in a leaning-down sort of kindness. You got none of that what-can-I-do-for-you-my-poor-child-look in you."

Her effusiveness embarrassed him.

"You make too much out of nothing."

"Nothing?" Her eyes were misty with emotion. "I was something wild up in the air, and I couldn't get hold of myself all alone, and you—you made me for a person."

"I cannot tell you how it affects me that in some way I do not understand I have been the means of bringing release to you. Of course," he added quickly, "I was only an instrument, not a cause. Just as a spade which digs the ground is not a cause of the fertility of the soil or of the lovely flowers which spring forth. I cannot get away from the poetic, the religious experience which has so unexpectedly overtaken me."

She listened to him in silent wonder. How different he was from the college people she had met at luncheon that day!

"I can't put it in words," she fumbled, "but I owe it to you, this confession. I can't help it. I used to hate so the educated! 'Why should they know everything, and me nothing?' it cried in me. 'Here I'm dying to learn, to be something, and they holding tight all the learning like misers hiding gold.'"

§ 7

President Irvine did not answer. After a while he began talking in his calm voice of his dream of democracy in education, of the plans under way for the founding of the new school.

"I see it all!" She leaped to her feet under the inspiration of his words. "This new school is not to be only for the higher-ups by the higher-ups. It's to be for everybody—the tailor and the fish-pedlar and the butcher. And the teachers are not to be professors, talking to us down from their heads, but living people, talking out of their hearts. It's to be what there never yet was in this country—a school for the people."

President Irvine had the sensation of being swept out of himself upon strange, sunlit shores. The bleak land of merely intellectual perception lay behind him. Her ardour, her earnestness broke through the habitual restraint of the Anglo-Saxon.

"Let me read you part of my lecture on the new school," he said, the contagion of her enthusiasm vibrant in his low voice. "Teachers, above all others, have occasion to be distressed when the earlier idealism of welcome to the oppressed is treated as a weak sentimentalism, when sympathy for the unfortunate and those who have not had a fair chance is regarded as a weak indulgence fatal to efficiency. The new school must aim to make up to the disinherited masses by conscious instruction, by the development of personal power for the loss of external opportunities consequent upon the passing of our pioneer days. Otherwise, power is likely to pass more and more into the hands of the wealthy, and we shall end with the same alliance between intellectual and artistic culture and economic power due to riches which has been the curse of every civilization in the past, and which our fathers in their democratic idealism thought this nation was to put an end to."

"Grand!" she cried, clapping her hands ecstatically. "Your language is a little too high over my head for me to understand what you're talking about, but I feel I know what you mean to say. You mean, in the new school, America is to be America, after all." Eyes tense, brilliant, held his. "I'll give you an advice," she went on. "Translate your lecture in plain words like they translate things from Russian into English, or English into Russian. If you want your new school to be for the people, so you got to begin by talking in the plain words of the people. You got to feel out your thoughts from the heart and not from the head."

Her words were like bullets that shot through the static security of his traditional past.

"Perhaps I can learn from you how to be simple."

"Sure! I feel I can learn you how to put flesh and blood into your words so that everybody can feel your thoughts close to the heart." The gesticulating hands swam before him like waves of living flame. "Stand before your eyes the people, the dumb, hungry people—hungry for knowledge. You got that knowledge. And when you talk in that high-headed lecture language, it's like you threw stones to those who are hungry for bread."

Then they were both silent, lost in their thoughts. There was a new light in her eyes, new strength in her arms and fingers, when she rose to go.

"I shall never see the America which is to be," he said as he took her hand in parting; "it will not come in my day. But I have seen its soul like a free wild bird, beating its wings not against bars, but against the skies that the light might come through and reveal the earth to be."

She walked down the corridor and out of the building still under the spell of his presence. "Like a free wild bird! like a free wild bird!" sang in her heart.

She had nearly reached home when she became aware that tears were running down her cheeks, but they were tears of a soul filled to the brim—tears of vision and revelation. The glow of the setting sun illuminated the whole earth. She saw the soul beneath the starved, penny-pinched faces of the Ghetto. The raucous voices of the hucksters, the haggling women, the shrill cries of the children—all seemed to blend and fuse into one song of new dawn, of hope, of faith fulfilled.

"After all," she breathed in prayerful gratitude, "it is 'to the stars through difficulties.' A *meshugeneh* like me, a cook from Rosinsky's Restaurant burning her way up to the president for a friend!"

AN IMMIGRANT AMONG THE EDITORS

Ever since I began to read the American magazines one burning question has consumed me: why is it that only the thoughts of educated people are written up? Why shouldn't sometimes a servant girl or a janitress or a coal-heaver give his thoughts to the world? We who are forced to do the drudgery of the world, and who are considered ignorant because we have no time for school, could say a lot of new and different things, if only we had a chance to get a hearing.

Very rarely I'd come across a story about a shop-girl or a washerwoman. But they weren't real stories. They were twisted pictures of the way the higher-ups see us people. They weren't as we are. They were as unreal as the knowledge of the rich about the poor. Often I'd read those smooth-flowing stories about nothing at all, and I'd ask myself: why is it that so many of the educated, with nothing to say, know how to say that nothing with such an easy flow of words, while I, with something so aching to be said, can say nothing?

I was like a prison world full of choked-in voices, all beating in my brain to be heard. The minute I'd listen to one voice a million other voices would rush in crying for a hearing, till I'd get too excited and mixed up to know what or where.

Sometimes I'd see my brain as a sort of Hester Street junk-shop, where a million different things—rich up-town silks and velvets and the cheapest kind of rags—were thrown around in bunches. It seemed to me if I struggled from morning till night all my years I could never put order in my junk-shop brain.

Ach! If I only had an education, I used to think. It seemed to me that educated people were those who had their hearts and their heads so settled down in order that they could go on with quiet stillness to do anything they set out to do. They could take up one thought, one feeling at a time without getting the rest of themselves mixed up and excited over it. They had each thought, each feeling, laid out in separate shelves in their heads. So they could draw out one shelf of ideas while the rest of their ideas remained quiet and still in the orderly place inside of them.

With me my thoughts were not up in my head. They were in my hands and feet, in the thinnest nerves of my hair, in the flesh and blood of my whole body. Everything hurt in me when I tried to think; it was like struggling up towards something over me that I could never reach—like tearing myself out inch by inch from the roots of the earth—like suffering all pain of dying and being born.

And when I'd really work out a thought in words, I'd want to say it over and over a million times, for fear maybe I wasn't saying it strong enough. And I'd clutch at my few little words as a starving man clutches at crumbs. I could never sit back with the feeling that I had said what I wanted to say, like the educated people, who are sure of themselves when they say something. The real thing I meant remained inside of me for want of deeper, more burning words than I had yet found in the cold English language.

With all the confused unsureness of myself, I was absolutely sure I had great things in me. I felt that all I needed was the chance to reach the educated higher-ups, and all the big things in me would leap out quicker than lightning. But how was I to reach these American-born higher-ups when they were so much above me? I could never get into their colleges because I could never take the time to learn all the beginnings from school to pass their entrance examinations. And even if I had the time to study, I wasn't interested in grammar and arithmetic and dry history and still drier and deader literature about Chaucer and Marlowe. I was too much on fire trying to think out my own thoughts to get interested in the dust and ashes of dead and gone ones. And yet I was so crazy to reach those who had all that book-learning from school in their heads that I was always dreaming of the wonderful educated world that was over me.

Sometimes I'd wake up in the middle of the night and stare through the darkness at an imaginary world of educated people that would invite me in to share with them their feast of learning. I saw them sitting around a table talking high thoughts, all the wisdom of the ages flowing from lip to lip like living light. I saw just how they talked and how they looked, because once I had worked as a waitress in a professor's house. Their words were over my head, but the sound of their low voices went through me like music of all that I longed and dreamed and desired to be.

I used to hold myself tight-in, like a wooden dummy, when I passed them the food. My lips were tight together, my eyes half-closed, like a Chinaman's, as though I didn't see or hear anything but my one business of waiting on them. But all the time something in the choked stillness of me was crying out to them: "I'm no dummy of a servant. I want to be like you. I could be like all of you if I only had a chance."

"If I only had a chance" kept going round and round in my head.

"Make your chance," a still voice goaded me.

"If I could only write out my wonderful thoughts that fly away in the air I'd get myself a first place in America."

"No, go ahead. Think connectedly for one minute. Catch your crazy wild birds and bring them down to earth."

And so I pushed myself on to begin the adventure of writing out my thoughts.

But who'll print what I write? was my next bother.

In my evenings off I used to go to the library and kept looking and looking through all the magazines to see where I could get a start. At last I picked out three magazines that stood out plainly for their special interest in working people. I will call them *The Reformer*, *The People* and *Free Mankind*.

Free Mankind was a thin, white, educated-looking magazine, without covers, without pictures, without any advertising. It gave me the feeling when I looked through the pages that it was a head without a body. Most of the articles were high words in the air. I couldn't make out what they were talking about, but some of the editorials talked against paying rent. This at once got me on fire with interest, because all my life the people I knew were wearing out their years worrying for the rent. If this magazine was trying to put the landlords out of business, I was with it. So, fired by the inspiration of the moment, I rushed to see the editor of *Free Mankind*.

I don't remember how I ever pushed myself past the telephone girl and secretary, but I found myself talking face to face with a clean, cold, high-thinking head, Mr. Alfred Nott, editor-boss of *Free Mankind*. My burning enthusiasm turned into ice through all my bones as I looked into the terrible, clean face and cold eyes of this clean cold higher-up. But I heard my words rushing right to him like the words of a soap-box speaker who is so on fire with his thoughts that even the cold ones from up-town are forced to listen to him.

"I can put a lot of new life into your magazine," I said. "I have in me great new ideas about life, and I'm crazy to give them out to you. Your magazine is too much up in the head and not enough down on earth. It's all words, words, long-winded empty words in emptiness. Your articles are something like those long sermons about nothing, that put people to sleep. I can wake up your readers like lightning. I can make your magazine mean living things to living people."

The man fell back in his chair as if frightened. His mouth opened to speak, but no words came from his lips.

"What you tell us about not paying rent is good enough," I went on. "But you should tell us how to put an end to all that. I know enough about not having a place to sleep in to write you something that will wake up the dead. You're not excited enough with feelings when you write, because you live in a soft steam-heated place with plenty of money to pay for it. But the poor like me, with little rent, and drying out their heads worrying for that little, they feel what it is to be under the foot of those Cossacks, the landlords. In my stories I'd write for you, I'd get the readers so mad, they'd rush out and do something."

Even while I was yet talking, Mr. Nott slipped out of the chair and disappeared like a frightened rabbit. I could see him vanishing through the door before I could stop my flow of words. I looked about me in the empty room. I felt as if I'd been slapped in the face.

I ran out of the office with tears in my eyes. And I couldn't stop my crying in the street. So this is his Free Mankind! When a person comes to him with something real he runs away as from a madman. Here was a paper that would reform the world, and its boss wouldn't even listen to one of the people he was setting out to save.

But there were other magazines in America, I told myself. *The Reformer* flashed before my eyes, because I remember it said on the back page, "It speaks for the average man."

I found myself again face to face with an editor—John Blair, the great liberal, the friend of an American President, the starter of a new school that was to gather all the minds of the new world. With this man I thought I'd begin by asking him a question instead of rushing myself out to him in all my hungry eagerness.

"Mr. Blair," I demanded in a voice of choked-in quietness, "do you think that the educated people know it all?"

He looked at me for a long minute. His lips closed together, his eyes cool like a judge. I felt he looked me over to decide in what shelf I belonged in the filing bureau of his college head.

"No, my dear young woman. I don't say that educated people have a monopoly of knowledge, but they are the only ones that know how to use it."

"Then it's only the thoughts of educated people for your magazine," I cried disappointedly. "How about people like me with a lot to say but can't put it in fancy language? Isn't your new school to be different from the old colleges in that you want to bring out the new thoughts of new people like me? Wouldn't you want to give a person like me a chance in your magazine?"

"But can you express yourself logically, reasonably?"

"Logic—reason! Reason—logic!" I jumped from the chair with excitement. "That's why your magazine is so dull, so dead, because all your living thoughts die down in the ashes of dead logic. Reason and logic aren't life.

Hunger and desire are life. I know, because I'm burning up with it. With this hunger they paint pictures and write books and sing songs——"

"You Russians are full of interesting stuff. But you're so incoherent. You'd be no use to us unless you could learn to think clearly."

"I know my thoughts are all mixed up," I pleaded with educated quietness, "but it's only because I have so much to give and nobody wants it. Wouldn't it be better for your magazine to have my mixed-up aliveness instead of the cold logic from your college writers?"

He smiled down pityingly on me.

"I'm afraid that such a chaotic mind as yours would be useless to an intellectual journal. Good day."

Not crushed, but bitter and hard and with head high, I walked out of *The Reformer* office. Were all the magazines that set themselves up to save the world headed by such narrow-thinking tsars? Only to prove that all of them were run by some clique of college professors, I went to the office of *The People*.

Here the editor didn't run from me like a frightened rabbit or sting me with logic like John Blair. He cut short the interview by going over to the shelf and taking down a book which he handed to me with pitying kindness. "This will help you to think and maybe to write."

Out in the street, I gave a look at the book. It was Genung's "Psychology of Madness." It grew black and red before my eyes. So it's madness to want to give out my thoughts to the world? They turn me down like a crazy beggar only because I come to give them new ideas.

I threw the book away in the nearest ash can. But that word "madness" was to me like a red rag to a bull. I had to write now or go crazy with the wrath these reformers roused in me.

"What's my place in America?" I asked myself. "Must I remain a choked-in servant in somebody's kitchen or somebody's factory, or will I find a way to give out my thoughts to America?"

So what I wrote was the story of myself—myself lost in America.

It was like new air in my lungs to let myself loose on paper. But how could I get it to the American people? One thing I was sure of. I wasn't going to subject myself to another insult from those reform magazines. I don't know how it happened, but I picked out *Wharton's Magazine*, the most literary magazine of all those I looked over, simply because it looked so solidly high above the rest. My desperate need for a hearing made me bold. In my ragged coat and torn shoes I walked into that breath-taking rich office like a millionaire landlord with pockets full of rent money.

"Do you want something new and different for your magazine?" I asked with the low voice and the high head of an American-born.

Friendly eyes turned on me. "We're always seeking something new and different. Have you got it?"

I looked right into the friendly eyes. This was Mr. Robert Reeves, the editor. He had the clean, well-dressed look of the born higher-up. But how different from those others! His face was human. And there was a shine in the eyes that warmed me.

"I'm an immigrant," I said. "I have worked in kitchens, factories and sweatshops. I'm dying away with the loneliness of my thoughts, so I wrote myself out in a story."

He snatched up the papers and began to read. A quick light flashed into his eyes. Then he turned to me.

"I can see you have something original. But I can't decide just now. You'll hear from me as soon as I have read it through."

I could hardly walk the street for excitement. My life hung on this man's answer. And it came two days later in a small envelope. He offered me two hundred dollars for my story.

I couldn't believe it wasn't a dream. And I rushed with the letter to his office. "You could have given me a hundred dollars, fifty, twenty-five, and it would have been to me a fortune. But two hundred—do you mean really to give that much to me?"

He chuckled to himself, and I rushed right on. "I thought New York was a den of thieves. The landlord robbing you with the rent, and the restaurants cheating the strength out of every bite of food you buy. And I thought the college higher-ups were only educated cowards with dish-water in their veins, scared to death of hungry people like me, scared to look at the face of suffering. Their logic and their reason—only how to use their book-learning brains to shut out their hearts—to make themselves deaf, dumb and blind to the cry of hunger and want knocking at their doors."

"Just because you felt all that so deeply you were able to put fire in your words."

A thousand windows of light burst open in me as I listened to him. I was like something choked for ages in the tight chains of ignorance and fear, breathing the first breath of free air. For the first time my eyes began to see, my ears began to hear, my heart began to understand the world's wonder and the beauty.

A great pity welled up in my heart for the Alfred Notts and the John Blairs whom I had so mercilessly condemned. Poor little-educated ones! Why did I fear them and envy them and hate them so for nothing? They were only little children putting on a long wooden face, playing teacher to the world. And I was a little scared child afraid of teacher—afraid they were grown-ups with the power to hurt me and shut me out from the fun of life.

Why wasn't I scared of Robert Reeves from the first minute? It was because he didn't frighten people with his highness. He didn't wear a wooden face of dignity. He was no reformer, no holy social worker—only a human being who loved people.

That one flash of understanding from Robert Reeves filled me with such enthusiasm for work that I shut myself off from the rest of the world and began turning out story after story.

Years passed. The only sign of success I became aware of was the increasing flood of mail that poured in on me. People who wanted to be writers asked me for literary help. People who imagined I was rolling in money sent me begging letters for aid. At the beginning I wanted to help them all. But I soon saw that I'd have to spend all my time answering the demands of foolish self-seekers who had nothing in common with me. And so I had to harden my heart against these time-wasting intruders.

One day, as I walked out of my house absorbed in one of the characters that I was writing about, someone stopped me. I looked up. A pale, thin, hungry-eyed young man asked timidly: "May I speak to you for a minute?" Then he told me that he had written a book, and that the publishers had turned it down, so he had printed it himself. "And I want your opinion," he pleaded, "because none of the critics would listen to me."

"I'm too busy," I said irritably. "If you had to print the book yourself it means it's no good."

"I thought you, who once had such a hard struggle, would remember—would understand."

"There's nothing to understand except that you killed yourself with the public." And I walked off.

I tried to resume the trend of my thoughts, but I could not think. The pale face, the hungry eyes, followed me accusingly in the street. "You who once struggled would understand" rang in my ears. And suddenly I realized how brutal I had been.

"But it's the merciless truth," I defended. Nobody could help him till he finds himself. Nobody helped me till I had found myself.

"No, I'm all wrong," another voice cried. "Robert Reeves helped me. I could never have helped myself all alone. You can only help yourself half the way. The other half is some Hand of God in the shape of a human contact."

Something hurt so deep in me I couldn't work that day. I couldn't sleep that night. The pale face and the hungry eyes kept staring at me through the darkness. I, who judged the Alfred Notts and the John Blairs—I saw myself condemned as one of them. I had let myself get so absorbed with the thoughts in my head that I ceased to have a heart for the people about me.

What would I not have given to see that young man and tell him how I suffered for my inhuman busy-business, which had shut my eyes to the hungry hands reaching up to me. But I never saw him again. And yet that man whom I had turned away like a beggar had brought me the life of a new awakening. He had made me aware that I could never contribute my deepest to America if I lost the friendly understanding of humanity that Robert Reeves had given me, if I lost the one precious thing that makes life real— the love for people, even if they are lost, wandering, crazy people.

AMERICA AND I

As one of the dumb, voiceless ones I speak. One of the millions of immigrants beating, beating out their hearts at your gates for a breath of understanding.

Ach! America! From the other end of the earth from where I came, America was a land of living hope, woven of dreams, aflame with longing and desire.

Choked for ages in the airless oppression of Russia, the Promised Land rose up—wings for my stifled spirit—sunlight burning through my darkness—freedom singing to me in my prison—deathless songs tuning prison bars into strings of a beautiful violin.

I arrived in America. My young, strong body, my heart and soul pregnant with the unlived lives of generations clamouring for expression.

What my mother and father and their mother and father never had a chance to give out in Russia, I would give out in America. The hidden sap of centuries would find release; colours that never saw light—songs that died unvoiced—romance that never had a chance to blossom in the black life of the Old World.

In the golden land of flowing opportunity I was to find my work that was denied me in the sterile village of my forefathers. Here I was to be free from the dead drudgery for bread that held me down in Russia. For the first time in America I'd cease to be a slave of the belly. I'd be a creator, a giver, a human being! My work would be the living joy of fullest self-expression.

But from my high visions, my golden hopes, I had to put my feet down on earth. I had to have food and shelter. I had to have the money to pay for it.

I was in America, among the Americans, but not of them. No speech, no common language, no way to win a smile of understanding from them, only my young, strong body and my untried faith. Only my eager, empty hands, and my full heart shining from my eyes!

God from the world! Here I was with so much richness in me, but my mind was not wanted without the language. And my body, unskilled, untrained, was not even wanted in the factory. Only one of two chances was left open to me: the kitchen, or minding babies.

My first job was as a servant in an Americanized family. Once, long ago, they came from the same village from where I came. But they were so well dressed, so well fed, so successful in America, that they were ashamed to remember their mother tongue.

"What were to be my wages?" I ventured timidly, as I looked up to the well-fed, well-dressed "American" man and woman.

They looked at me with a sudden coldness. What have I said to draw away from me their warmth? Was it so low from me to talk of wages? I shrank back into myself like a low-down bargainer. Maybe they're so high up in well-being they can't any more understand my low thoughts for money.

From his rich height the man preached down to me that I must not be so grabbing for wages. Only just landed from the ship and already thinking about money when I should be thankful to associate with "Americans."

The woman, out of her smooth, smiling fatness, assured me that this was my chance for a summer vacation in the country with her two lovely children. My great chance to learn to be a civilized being, to become an American by living with them.

So, made to feel that I was in the hands of American friends, invited to share with them their home, their plenty, their happiness, I pushed out from my head the worry for wages. Here was my first chance to begin my life in the sunshine after my long darkness. My laugh was all over my face as I said to them: "I'll trust myself to you. What I'm worth you'll give me." And I entered their house like a child by the hand.

The best of me I gave them. Their house cares were my house cares. I got up early. I worked till late. All that my soul hungered to give I put into the passion with which I scrubbed floors, scoured pots, and washed clothes. I was so grateful to mingle with the American people, to hear the music of the American language, that I never knew tiredness.

There was such a freshness in my brains and such a willingness in my heart that I could go on and on—not only with the work of the house, but work with my head—learning new words from the children, the grocer, the butcher, the iceman. I was not even afraid to ask for words from the policeman on the street. And every new word made me see new American things with American eyes. I felt like a Columbus, finding new worlds through every new word.

But words alone were only for the inside of me. The outside of me still branded me for a steerage immigrant. I had to have clothes to forget myself that I'm a stranger yet. And so I had to have money to buy these clothes.

The month was up. I was so happy! Now I'd have money. *My own, earned* money. Money to buy a new shirt on my back, shoes on my feet. Maybe yet an American dress and hat!

Ach! How high rose my dreams! How plainly I saw all that I would do with my visionary wages shining like a light over my head!

In my imagination I already walked in my new American clothes. How beautiful I looked as I saw myself like a picture before my eyes! I saw how I would throw away my immigrant rags tied up in my immigrant shawl. With money to buy—free money in my hands—I'd show them that I could look like an American in a day.

Like a prisoner in his last night in prison, counting the seconds that will free him from his chains, I trembled breathlessly for the minute I'd get the wages in my hand.

Before dawn I rose.

I shined up the house like a jewel-box.

I prepared breakfast and waited with my heart in my mouth for my lady and gentleman to rise. At last I heard them stirring. My eyes were jumping out of my head to them when I saw them coming in and seating themselves by the table.

Like a hungry cat rubbing up to its boss for meat, so I edged and simpered around them as I passed them the food. Without my will, like a beggar, my hand reached out to them.

The breakfast was over. And no word yet from my wages.

"Gottuniu!" I thought to myself. "Maybe they're so busy with their own things they forgot it's the day for my wages. Could they who have everything know what I was to do with my first American dollars? How could they, soaking in plenty, how could they feel the longing and the fierce hunger in me, pressing up through each visionary dollar? How could they know the gnawing ache of my avid fingers for the feel of my own, earned dollars? *My* dollars that I could spend like a free person. *My* dollars that would make me feel with everybody alike!"

Breakfast was long past.

Lunch came. Lunch past.

Oi-i weh! Not a word yet about my money.

It was near dinner. And not a word yet about my wages.

I began to set the table. But my head—it swam away from me. I broke a glass. The silver dropped from my nervous fingers. I couldn't stand it any longer. I dropped everything and rushed over to my American lady and gentleman.

"Oi weh! The money—my money—my wages!" I cried breathlessly.

Four cold eyes turned on me.

"Wages? Money?" The four eyes turned into hard stone as they looked me up and down. "Haven't you a comfortable bed to sleep, and three good meals a day? You're only a month here. Just came to America. And you already think about money. Wait till you're worth any money. What use are you without knowing English? You should be glad we keep you here. It's like a vacation for you. Other girls pay money yet to be in the country."

It went black for my eyes. I was so choked no words came to my lips. Even the tears went dry in my throat.

I left. Not a dollar for all my work!

For a long, long time my heart ached and ached like a sore wound. If murderers would have robbed me and killed me it wouldn't have hurt me so much. I couldn't think through my pain. The minute I'd see before me how they looked at me, the words they said to me—then everything began to bleed in me. And I was helpless.

For a long, long time the thought of ever working in an "American" family made me tremble with fear, like the fear of wild wolves. No—never again would I trust myself to an "American" family, no matter how fine their language and how sweet their smile.

It was blotted out in me, all trust in friendship from "Americans." But the life in me still burned to live. The hope in me still craved to hope. In darkness, in dirt, in hunger and want, but only to live on!

There had been no end to my day—working for the "American" family.

Now rejecting false friendships from higher-ups in America, I turned back to the ghetto. I worked on a hard bench with my own kind on either side of me. I knew before I began what my wages were to be. I knew what my hours were to be. And I knew the feeling of the end of the day.

From the outside my second job seemed worse than the first. It was in a sweat-shop of a Delancey Street basement, kept up by an old, wrinkled woman that looked like a black witch of greed. My work was sewing on buttons. While the morning was still dark I walked into a dark basement. And darkness met me when I turned out of the basement.

Day after day, week after week, all the contact I got with America was handling dead buttons. The money I earned was hardly enough to pay for bread and rent. I didn't have a room to myself. I didn't even have a bed. I slept on a mattress on the floor in a rat-hole of a room occupied by a dozen other immigrants. I was always hungry—oh, so hungry! The scant meals I could afford only sharpened my appetite for real food. But I felt myself better off than working in the "American" family, where I had three good meals a day and a bed to myself. With all the hunger and darkness of the sweat-shop,

I had at least the evening to myself. And all night was mine. When all were asleep, I used to creep up on the roof of the tenement and talk out my heart in silence to the stars in the sky.

"Who am I? What am I? What do I want with my life? Where is America? Is there an America? What is this wilderness in which I'm lost?"

I'd hurl my questions and then think and think. And I could not tear it out of me, the feeling that America must be somewhere, somehow—only I couldn't find it—*my America*, where I would work for love and not for a living. I was like a thing following blindly after something far off in the dark!

"Oi weh!" I'd stretch out my hand up in the air. "My head is so lost in America! What's the use of all my working if I'm not in it? Dead buttons is not me."

Then the busy season started in the shop. The mounds of buttons grew and grew. The long day stretched out longer. I had to begin with the buttons earlier and stay with them till later in the night. The old witch turned into a huge greedy maw for wanting more and more buttons.

For a glass of tea, for a slice of herring over black bread, she would buy us up to stay another and another hour, till there seemed no end to her demands.

One day, the light of self-assertion broke into my cellar darkness.

"I don't want the tea. I don't want your herring," I said with terrible boldness. "I only want to go home. I only want the evening to myself!"

"You fresh mouth, you!" cried the old witch. "You learned already too much in America. I want no clock-watchers in my shop. Out you go!"

I was driven out to cold and hunger. I could no longer pay for my mattress on the floor. I no longer could buy the bite in the mouth. I walked the streets. I knew what it is to be alone in a strange city among strangers.

But I laughed through my tears. So I learned too much already in America because I wanted the whole evening to myself? Well, America has yet to teach me still more: how to get not only the whole evening to myself, but a whole day a week like the American workers.

That sweat-shop was a bitter memory but a good school. It fitted me for a regular factory. I could walk in boldly and say I could work at something, even if it was only sewing on buttons.

Gradually, I became a trained worker. I worked in a light, airy factory, only eight hours a day. My boss was no longer a sweater and a blood-squeezer.

The first freshness of the morning was mine. And the whole evening was mine. All day Sunday was mine.

Now I had better food to eat. I slept on a better bed. Now, I even looked dressed up like the American-born. But inside of me I knew that I was not yet an American. I choked with longing when I met an American-born, and I couldn't say nothing.

Something cried dumb in me. I couldn't help it. I didn't know what it was I wanted. I only knew I wanted. I wanted. Like the hunger in the heart that never gets food.

An English class for foreigners started in our factory. The teacher had such a good, friendly face, her eyes looked so understanding, as though she could see right into my heart. So I went to her one day for an advice:

"I don't know what is with me the matter," I began. "I have no rest in me. I never yet done what I want."

"What is it you want to do, child?" she asked me.

"I want to do something with my head, my feelings. All day long, only with my hands I work."

"First you must learn English." She patted me as though I was not yet grown up. "Put your mind on that, and then we'll see."

So for a time I learned the language. I could almost begin to think with English words in my head. But in my heart still hurt the emptiness. I burned to give, to give something, to do something, to be something. The dead work with my hands was killing me. My work left only hard stones on my heart.

Again I went to our factory teacher and cried out to her: "I know already to read and write the English language, but I can't put it into words what I want. What is it in me so different that can't come out?"

She smiled at me down from her calmness as if I were a little bit out of my head. "What *do you want* to do?"

"I feel. I see. I hear. And I want to think it out. But I'm like dumb in me. I only feel I'm different—different from everybody."

She looked at me close and said nothing for a minute. "You ought to join one of the social clubs of the Women's Association," she advised.

"What's the Women's Association?" I implored greedily.

"A group of American women who are trying to help the working-girl find herself. They have a special department for immigrant girls like you."

I joined the Women's Association. On my first evening there they announced a lecture: "The Happy Worker and His Work," by the Welfare director of the United Mills Corporation.

"Is there such a thing as a happy worker at his work?" I wondered. "Happiness is only by working at what you love. And what poor girl can ever find it to work at what she loves?" My old dreams about my America rushed through my mind. Once I thought that in America everybody works for love. Nobody has to worry for a living. Maybe this welfare man came to show me the *real* America that till now I sought in vain.

With a lot of polite words the head lady of the Women's Association introduced a higher-up that looked like the king of kings of business. Never before in my life did I ever see a man with such a sureness in his step, such power in his face, such friendly positiveness in his eye as when he smiled upon us.

"Efficiency is the new religion of business," he began. "In big business houses, even in up-to-date factories, they no longer take the first comer and give him any job that happens to stand empty. Efficiency begins at the employment office. Experts are hired for the one purpose, to find out how best to fit the worker to his work. It's economy for the boss to make the worker happy." And then he talked a lot more on efficiency in educated language that was over my head.

I didn't know exactly what it meant—efficiency—but if it was to make the worker happy at his work, then that's what I had been looking for since I came to America. I only felt from watching him that he was happy by his job. And as I looked on this clean, well-dressed, successful one, who wasn't ashamed to say he rose from an office-boy, it made me feel that I, too, could lift myself up for a person.

He finished his lecture, telling us about the Vocational Guidance Centre that the Women's Association started.

The very next evening I was at the Vocational Guidance Centre. There I found a young, college-looking woman. Smartness and health shining from her eyes! She, too, looked as if she knew her way in America. I could tell at the first glance: here is a person that is happy by what she does.

"I feel you'll understand me," I said right away.

She leaned over with pleasure in her face: "I hope I can."

"I want to work by what's in me. Only, I don't know what's in me. I only feel I'm different."

She gave me a quick, puzzled look from the corner of her eyes. "What are you doing now?"

"I'm the quickest shirtwaist hand on the floor. But my heart wastes away by such work. I think and think, and my thoughts can't come out."

"Why don't you think out your thoughts in shirtwaists? You could learn to be a designer. Earn more money."

"I don't want to look on waists. If my hands are sick from waists, how could my head learn to put beauty into them?"

"But you must earn your living at what you know, and rise slowly from job to job."

I looked at her office sign: "Vocational Guidance." "What's your vocational guidance?" I asked. "How to rise from job to job—how to earn more money?"

The smile went out from her eyes. But she tried to be kind yet. "What *do* you want?" she asked, with a sigh of lost patience.

"I want America to want me."

She fell back in her chair, thunderstruck with my boldness. But yet, in a low voice of educated self-control, she tried to reason with me:

"You have to *show* that you have something special for America before America has need of you."

"But I never had a chance to find out what's in me, because I always had to work for a living. Only, I feel it's efficiency for America to find out what's in me so different, so I could give it out by my work."

Her eyes half closed as they bored through me. Her mouth opened to speak, but no words came from her lips. So I flamed up with all that was choking in me like a house on fire:

"America gives free bread and rent to criminals in prison. They got grand houses, with sunshine, fresh air, doctors and teachers, even for the crazy ones. Why don't they have free boarding-schools for immigrants—strong people—willing people? Here you see us burning up with something different, and America turns its head away from us."

Her brows lifted and dropped down. She shrugged her shoulders away from me with the look of pity we give to cripples and hopeless lunatics.

"America is no Utopia. First you must become efficient in earning a living before you can indulge in your poetic dreams."

I went away from the vocational guidance office with all the air out of my lungs. All the light out of my eyes. My feet dragged after me like dead wood.

Till now there had always lingered a rosy veil of hope over my emptiness, a hope that a miracle would happen. I would open up my eyes some day and suddenly find the America of my dreams. As a young girl hungry for love sees always before her eyes the picture of lover's arms around her, so I saw always in my heart the vision of Utopian America.

But now I felt that the America of my dreams never was and never could be. Reality had hit me on the head as with a club. I felt that the America that I sought was nothing but a shadow—an echo—a chimera of lunatics and crazy immigrants.

Stripped of all illusion, I looked about me. The long desert of wasting days of drudgery stared me in the face. The drudgery that I had lived through, and the endless drudgery still ahead of me rose over me like a withering wilderness of sand. In vain were all my cryings, in vain were all frantic efforts of my spirit to find the living waters of understanding for my perishing lips. Sand, sand was everywhere. With every seeking, every reaching out I only lost myself deeper and deeper in a vast sea of sand.

I knew now the American language. And I knew now, if I talked to the Americans from morning till night, they could not understand what the Russian soul of me wanted. They could not understand *me* any more than if I talked to them in Chinese. Between my soul and the American soul were worlds of difference that no words could bridge over. What was that difference? What made the Americans so far apart from me?

I began to read the American history. I found from the first pages that America started with a band of courageous Pilgrims. They had left their native country as I had left mine. They had crossed an unknown ocean and landed in an unknown country, as I.

But the great difference between the first Pilgrims and me was that they expected to make America, build America, create their own world of liberty. I wanted to find it ready-made.

I read on. I delved deeper down into the American history. I saw how the Pilgrim Fathers came to a rocky desert country, surrounded by Indian savages on all sides. But undaunted, they pressed on—through danger—through famine, pestilence, and want—they pressed on. They did not ask the Indians for sympathy, for understanding. They made no demands on anybody, but on their own indomitable spirit of persistence.

And I—I was for ever begging a crumb of sympathy, a gleam of understanding from strangers who could not sympathize, who could not understand.

I, when I encountered a few savage Indian scalpers, like the old witch of the sweat-shop, like my "Americanized" countryman, who cheated me of my wages—I, when I found myself on the lonely, untrodden path through which all seekers of the new world must pass, I lost heart and said: "There is no America!"

Then came a light—a great revelation! I saw America—a big idea—a deathless hope—a world still in the making. I saw that it was the glory of America that it was not yet finished. And I, the last comer, had her share to give, small or great, to the making of America, like those Pilgrims who came in the *Mayflower*.

Fired up by this revealing light, I began to build a bridge of understanding between the American-born and myself. Since their life was shut out from such as me, I began to open up my life and the lives of my people to them. And life draws life. In only writing about the Ghetto I found America.

Great chances have come to me. But in my heart is always a deep sadness. I feel like a man who is sitting down to a secret table of plenty, while his near ones and dear ones are perishing before his eyes. My very joy in doing the work I love hurts me like secret guilt, because all about me I see so many with my longings, my burning eagerness, to do and to be, wasting their days in drudgery they hate, merely to buy bread and pay rent. And America is losing all that richness of the soul.

The Americans of to-morrow, the America that is every day nearer coming to be, will be too wise, too open-hearted, too friendly-handed, to let the least last-comer at their gates knock in vain with his gifts unwanted.

A BED FOR THE NIGHT

A drizzling rain had begun to fall. I was wet and chilled to the bone. I had just left the free ward of a hospital, where I had been taken when ill with the flu. It was good to be home again! Even though what I called home were but the dim, narrow halls of a lodging-house. With a sigh of relief, I dropped my suitcase in the vestibule.

As the door swung open, the landlady met me with: "Your room is taken. Your things are in the cellar."

"My room?" I stammered, white with fear.

"Oh no—please, Mrs. Pelz!"

"I got a chance to rent your room at such a good price, I couldn't afford to hold it."

"But you promised to keep it for me while I was away. And I paid you for it——"

"The landlord raised me my rent and I got to get it out from the roomers," she defended. "I got four hungry mouths to feed——"

"But maybe I would have paid you a little more," I pleaded. "If you had only told me. I have to go back to work to-day. How can I get another room at a moment's notice?"

"We all got to look out for ourselves. I am getting more than twice as much as you paid me from this new lodger," she finished triumphantly. "And no housekeeping privileges."

"You must give me time!" My voice rose into a shriek. "You can't put a girl out into the street at a moment's notice. There are laws in America——"

"There are no laws for roomers."

"No law for roomers?" All my weakness and helplessness rushed out of me in a fury of rebellion. "No law for roomers?"

"I could have put your things out in the street when your week was up. But being you were sick, I was kind enough to keep them in the cellar. But your room is taken," she said with finality. "I got to let my rooms to them as pay the most. I got to feed my own children first. I can't carry the whole world on my back."

I tried to speak. But no voice came to my lips. I felt struck with a club on the head. I could only stare at her. And I must have been staring for some time without seeing her, for I had not noticed she had gone till I heard a voice from the upper stairs, "Are you still here?"

"Oh—yes—yes—I—I—am—going—go-ing." I tried to rouse my stunned senses, which seemed struck to the earth.

"There's no money in letting rooms to girls," my landlady continued, as she came down to open the door for me. "They're always cooking, or washing, or ironing and using out my gas. This new roomer I never hear nor see except in the morning when he goes to work and at night when he comes to sleep."

I staggered out in a bewildered daze. I leaned against the cold iron lamp-post. It seemed so kind, so warm. Even the chill, drizzling rain beating on my face was almost human. Slowly, my numbed brain began to recollect where I was. Where should I turn? To whom? I faced an endless maze of endless streets. All about me strangers—seas of jostling strangers. I was alone—shelterless!

All that I had suffered in lodging-houses rushed over me. I had never really lived or breathed like a free, human being. My closed door assured me no privacy. I lived in constant dread of any moment being pounced upon by my landlady for daring to be alive. I dared not hang out my clothes on a line in the fresh air. I was forced to wash and dry them stealthily, at night, over chairs and on my trunk. I was under the same restraint when I did my simple cooking although I paid dearly for the gas I used.

This ceaseless strain of don't move here and don't step there was far from my idea of home. But still it was shelter from the streets. I had almost become used to it. I had almost learned not to be crushed by it. Now, I was shut out—kicked out like a homeless dog.

All thought of reporting at my office left my mind. I walked and walked, driven by despair. Tears pressed in my throat, but my eyes were dry as sand.

I tried to struggle out of my depression. I looked through the furnished room sections of the city. There were no cheap rooms to be had. The prices asked for the few left were ten, twelve and fifteen dollars a week.

I earn twenty-five dollars a week as a stenographer. I am compelled to dress neatly to hold down my job. And with clothes and food so high, how could I possibly pay more than one-third of my salary for rent?

In my darkness I saw a light—a vision of the settlement. As an immigrant I had joined one of the social clubs there, and I remembered there was a residence somewhere in that building for the workers. Surely they would take me in till I had found a place to live.

"I'm in such trouble!" I stammered, as I entered the office of the head resident. "My landlady put me out because I couldn't pay the raise in rent."

"The housing problem is appalling," Miss Ward agreed with her usual professional friendliness. "I wish I could let you stay with us, my child, but our place is only for social workers."

"Where should I go?" I struggled to keep back my tears. "I'm so terribly alone."

"Now—now, dear child," Miss Ward patted my shoulder encouragingly. "You mustn't give way like that. Of course, I'll give you the addresses of mothers of our neighbourhood."

One swift glance at the calm, well-fed face and I felt instantly that Miss Ward had never known the terror of homelessness.

"You know, dear, I want to help you all I can," smiled Miss Ward, trying to be kind, "and I'm always glad when my girls come to me."

"What was the use of my coming to you?" I was in no mood for her make-believe settlement smile. "If you don't take me in, aren't you pushing me in the street—joining hands with my landlady?"

"Why—my dear!" The mask of smiling kindness dropped from Miss Ward's face. Her voice cooled. "Surely you will find a room in this long list of addresses I am giving you."

I went to a dozen places. It was the same everywhere. No rooms were to be had at the price I could afford.

Crushed again and again, the habit of hope still asserted itself. I suddenly remembered there was one person from whom I was almost sure of getting help—an American woman who had befriended me while still an immigrant in the factory. Her money had made it possible for me to take up the stenographic course. Full of renewed hope, I sped along the streets. My buoyant faith ever expectant could think of one outcome only.

Mrs. Olney had just finished dictating to her secretary, when the maid ushered me into the luxurious library.

"How good it is to see you! What can I do for you?" The touch of Mrs. Olney's fine hand, the sound of her lovely voice was like the warming breath of sunshine to a frozen thing. A choking came in my throat. Tears blinded me.

"If it wasn't a case of life and death, I wouldn't have bothered you so early in the morning."

"What's the trouble, my child?" Mrs. Olney was all concern.

"I can't stand it any longer! Get me a place to live!" And I told her of my experiences with my landlady and my hopeless room-hunting.

"I have many young friends who are in just your plight," Mrs. Olney consoled. "And I'm sending them all to the Better Housing Bureau."

I felt as though a powerful lamp went out suddenly within my soul. A sharp chill seized me. The chasm that divides those who have and those who have not yawned between us. The face I had loved and worshipped receded and grew dim under my searching gaze.

Here was a childless woman with a houseful of rooms to herself. Here was a philanthropist who gave thousands of dollars to help the poor. And here I tried to tell her that I was driven out into the street—shelterless. And her answer to my aching need was, "The Better Housing Bureau."

Again I turned to the unfeeling glare of the streets. A terrible loneliness bled in my heart. Such tearing, grinding pain was dragging me to the earth! I could barely hold myself up on my feet. "Ach! Only for a room to rest!" And I staggered like a dizzy drunkard to the Better Housing Bureau.

At the waiting-room I paused in breathless admiration. The soft greys and blues of the walls and hangings, the deep-seated divans, the flowers scattered in effective profusion, soothed and rested me like silent music. Even the smoothly fitting gown of the housing specialist seemed almost part of the colour scheme.

As I approached the mahogany desk I felt shabby—uncomfortable in this flawless atmosphere, but I managed somehow to tell of my need. I had no sooner explained the kind of room I could afford than the lady requested the twenty-five cents registration fee.

"I want to see the room first," I demanded.

"All our applicants pay in advance."

"I have only a two-dollar bill, and I don't get my pay till Monday."

"Oh, that's all right. I'll change it," she offered obligingly. And she took my one remaining bill.

"Where were you born? What is your religion?"

"I came for a room and not to be inquisitioned," I retorted.

"We are compelled to keep statistics of all our applicants."

Resentfully, I gave her the desired information, and with the addresses she had given me I recommenced my search. At the end of another futile hour of room-hunting there was added to the twenty-five cents registration fee an expense of fifteen cents for car fare. And I was still homeless.

I had been expecting to hear from my sister who had married a prosperous merchant and whom I hadn't seen for years. In my agitation I had forgotten to ask for my mail, and I went back to see about it. A telegram had come, stating my sister was staying at the Astor and I was to meet her there for lunch.

I hastened to her. For although she was now rich and comfortable, I felt that after all she was my sister and she would help me out.

"How shabby you look!" She cast a disapproving glance at me from head to foot. "Couldn't you dress decently to meet me, when you knew I was staying at this fashionable hotel?"

I told her of my plight.

"Why not go to a hotel till you find a suitable room?" she blandly advised.

My laughter sounded unreal so loud it was, as I reminded her, "Before the French Revolution, when the starving people came to the queen's palace clamouring for bread, the queen innocently exclaimed, 'Why don't they eat cake?'"

"How disagreeable you are! You think of no one but yourself. I've come here for a little change, to get away from my own troubles, and here you come with your hatefulness."

I hadn't known the relief of laughter, but now that I was started I couldn't stop, no more than I could stop staring at her. I tried to associate this new being of silks and jewels with her who had worked side by side with me in the factory.

"How you act! I think you're crazy," she admonished, and glanced at her wrist-watch. "I'm late for my appointment with the manicurist. I have to have my nails done after this dusty railway trip."

And I had been surprised at the insensate settlement worker, at my uncomprehending American friend who knew not the meaning of want. Yet here was my own sister, my own flesh and blood, reared in the same ghetto, nurtured in the same poverty, ground in the same sweat-shop treadmill, and because she had a few years of prosperity, because she ate well and dressed well and was secure, she was deaf to my cry.

Where I could hope for understanding, where I could turn for shelter, where I was to lay my head that very night, I knew not. But this much suddenly came to me, I was due to report for work that day. I was shut out on every side, but there in my office at least awaited me the warmth and sunshine of an assured welcome. My employer would understand and let me take off the remainder of the day to continue my search.

I found him out, and instead awaiting me was a pile of mail which he had left word I should attend to. The next hour was torture. My power of concentration had deserted me. I tapped the keys of my typewriter with my fingers, but my brain was torn with worry, my nerves ready to snap. The day was nearly spent. Night was coming on and I had no place to lay my head.

I was finishing the last of the letters when he came. After a friendly greeting he turned to the letters. I dared not interrupt until the mail was signed.

"Girl! What's wrong? That's not like you!" He stared at me. "There are a dozen mistakes in each letter."

A blur. Everything seemed to twist and turn around me. Red and black spots blinded me. A clenched hand pounded his desk, and I heard a voice that seemed to come from me—scream like a lunatic. "I have no home—no home—not even a bed for the night!"

Then all I remember is the man's kindly tone as he handed me a glass of water. "Are you feeling better?" he asked.

"My landlady put me out," I said between laboured breaths. "Oh-h, I'm so lonely! Not a place to lay my head!"

I saw him fumble for his pocket-book and look at me strangely. His burning gaze seemed to strip me naked—pierce me through and through from head to foot. Something hurt so deep I choked with shame. I seized my hat and coat and ran out.

It was getting dark when I reached the entrance of Central Park. Exhausted, I dropped to the nearest bench. I didn't even know I was crying.

"Are you lonely, little one?" A hand slipped around my waist and a dapper young chap moved closer. "Are you lonely?" he repeated.

I let him talk. I knew he had nothing real to offer, but I was so tired, so ready to drop the burden of my weary body that I had no resistance in me. "There's no place for me," I thought to myself. "Everyone shuts me out. What difference what becomes of me? Who cares?"

My head dropped to his shoulder. And the cry broke from me, "I have no place to sleep to-night."

"Sleep?" I could feel him draw in his breath and a blood-shot gleam leaped into his eyes. "You should worry. I'll take care of that."

He flashed a roll of bills tauntingly. "How about it, kiddo? Can you change me a twenty-dollar bill?"

As his other hand reached for me, I wrenched loose from him as from the cloying touch of pitch. "I wish I were that kind! I wish I were your kind! But I'm not!"

His hands dropped from the touch of me as though his flesh was scorched, and I found I was alone.

I walked again. At the nearest public telephone office I called up the women's hotels. None had a room left for less than two dollars. My remaining cash was forty cents short. The Better Housing Bureau had robbed me of my last hope of shelter.

I passed Fifth Avenue and Park Avenue mansions. Many were closed, standing empty. I began counting the windows, the rooms. Hundreds and hundreds of empty rooms, hundreds and hundreds of luxuriously furnished homes, and I homeless—shut out. I felt I was abandoned by God and man and no one cared if I perished or went mad. I had a fresh sense why the spirit of revolution was abroad in the land.

Blindly I retraced my steps to the park bench. I saw and felt nothing but a devouring sense of fear. It suddenly came over me that I was not living in a world of human beings, but in a jungle of savages who gorged themselves with food, gorged themselves with rooms, while I implored only a bed for the night. And I implored in vain.

I felt the chaos and destruction of the good and the beautiful within me and around me. The sight of people who lived in homes and ate three meals a day filled me with the fury of hate. The wrongs and injustices of the hungry and the homeless of all past ages burst from my soul like the smouldering lava of a blazing volcano. Earth-quakes of rebellion raced through my body and brain. I fell prone against the bench and wept, not tears, but blood.

"Move along! No loitering here!" The policeman's club tapped me on the shoulder. Then a woman stopped and bent over me.

I couldn't move. I couldn't lift my head.

"Tell your friend to cut out the sob-stuff," the officer continued, flourishing his club authoritatively. "On your way, both of youse. Y'know better than to loaf around here, Mag."

The woman put her hand on mine in a friendly little gesture of protection. "Leave her alone! Can't you see she's all in? I'll take care of her."

Her touch filled me with the warmth of shelter. I didn't know who or what she was, but I trusted her.

"Poor kid! What ails her? It's a rough world all alone."

There was no pity in her tone, but comprehension, fellowship. From childhood I'd had my friendships and many were dear to me. But this woman, without a word, without a greeting, had sounded the depths of understanding that I never knew existed. Even as I looked up at her she lifted me from the bench and almost carried me through the arbour of trees to the park entrance. My own mother couldn't have been more gentle. For a moment it seemed to me as though the spirit of my dead mother had risen from her grave in the guise of this unknown friend.

Only once the silence between us was broken. "Down in your luck, kid?" Her grip tightened on my arm. "I've been there myself. I know all about it."

She knew so well, what need had she of answer. The refrain came back to me: "Only themselves understand themselves and the likes of themselves, as souls only understand souls."

In a darkened side street we paused in front of a brown stone house with shutters drawn.

"Here we are! Now for some grub! I'll bet a nickel you ain't ate all day." She vaulted the rickety stairs two at a time and led the way into her little room. With a gay assertiveness she planted me into her one comfortable chair, attempting no apology for her poverty—a poverty that winked from every corner and could not be concealed. Flinging off her street clothes, she donned a crimson kimono, and rummaged through her soap-box in which her cooking things were kept. She wrung her hands with despair as though she suffered because she couldn't change herself into food.

Ah! the magic of love! It was only tea and toast and an outer crust of cheese she offered—but she offered it with the bounty of a princess. Only the kind look in her face and the smell of the steaming tray as she handed it to me— and I was filled before I touched the food to my lips. Somehow this woman who had so little had fed me as people with stuffed larders never could.

Under the spell of a hospitality so real that it hurt like divine, beautiful things hurt, I felt ashamed of my hysterical worries. I looked up at her and marvelled. She was so full of God-like grace—and so unconscious of it!

Not until she had tucked the covers warmly around me did I realize that I was occupying the only couch she had.

"But where will you sleep?" I questioned.

A funny little laugh broke from her. "I should worry where I sleep."

"It's so snug and comfy," I yawned, my eyes heavy with fatigue. "It's good to take from you——"

"Take? Aw, dry up, kid! You ain't taking nothing," she protested, embarrassed. "Tear off some sleep and forget it."

"I'll get close to the wall and make room for you," I murmured as I dropped off to sleep.

When I woke up I found, to my surprise, the woman was sleeping in a chair with a shawl wrapped around her like a huge statue. The half of the bed which she had left for me had remained untouched.

"You were sleeping so sound I didn't want to wake you," she said as she hurried to prepare the breakfast.

I rose, refreshed, restored—sane. It was more than gratitude that rushed out of my heart to her. I felt I belonged to someone, I had found home at last.

As I was ready to leave for work I turned to her. "I am coming back to-night," I said.

She fell back of a sudden as though I had struck her. From the quick pain that shone in her face I knew I had hurt something deep within her. Her eyes met mine in a fixed gaze but she did not see me, but stared through me into the vacancy of space. She seemed to have forgotten my presence, and when she spoke her voice was like that of one in a trance. "You don't know what you're asking. I—ain't—no good."

"You no good? God from the world! Where would I have been without you? Even my own sister shut me out. Of them all, you alone opened the door and spread for me all you had."

"I ain't so stuck on myself as the *good* people, although I was as good as any of them at the start. But the first time I got into trouble, instead of helping me, they gave me the marble stare and the frozen heart and drove me to the bad."

I looked closely at her, at the dyed hair, the rouged lips, the defiant look of the woman driven by the Pharisees from the steps of the temple. Then I saw beneath. It was as though her body dropped away from her and there stood revealed her soul—the sorrows that gave her understanding—the shame and the heartbreak that she turned into love.

"What is good or bad?" I challenged. "All I know is that I was hungry and you fed me. Shelterless and you sheltered me. Broken in spirit and you made me whole——"

"That stuff's all right, but you're better off out of here."

I started towards her in mute protest.

"Don't touch me," she cried. "Can't you see—the smut all over me? Ain't it in my face?"

Her voice broke. And like one possessed of sudden fury, she seized me by the shoulder and shoved me out.

As the door slammed I heard sobbing—loosened torrents of woe. I sank to my knees. A light not of this earth poured through the door that had shut on me. A holiness enveloped me.

This woman had changed the world for me. I could love the people I had hated yesterday. There was that something new in me, a light that the dingiest rooming house could not dim nor all the tyranny of the landlady shut out.

Vague, half remembered words flashed before me in letters of fire. "Despised and rejected of men: a woman of sorrows acquainted with grief."

DREAMS AND DOLLARS

Spring was in the air. But such radiant, joyous spring as one coming out of the dark shadows of the ghetto never could dream. Earth and sky seemed to sing with the joy of an unceasing holiday. Rebecca Yudelson felt as though she had suddenly stepped into fairyland, where the shadow of sorrow or sickness, where the black blight of poverty had never been.

An ecstasy of wonder and longing shone from her hungry, young eyes as she gazed at the luxurious dwellings. Such radiance of colour! Fruits, flowers and real orange-trees! Beauty and plenty! Each house outshone the other in beauty and plenty.

Fresh from the East Side tenements, worn from the nerve-racking grind of selling ribbons at the Five and Ten Cent Store, the residential section of Los Angeles was like a magic world of romance too perfect to be real. She had often seen the Fifth Avenue palaces of the New York millionaires when she had treated herself to a bus ride on a holiday. But nothing she had ever seen before compared with this glowing splendour.

"And in one of these mansions of sunshine and roses my own sister lives!" she breathed. "How could Minnie get used to so much free space and sunshine for every day?"

Ten years since Minnie had left Delancey Street. Ten years' freedom from the black worry for bread. There must have come a new sureness in her step, a new joy of life in her every movement. And to think that Abe Shmukler from cloaks and suits had bought her and brought her to this new world!

Rebecca wondered if her sister ever thought back to Felix Weinberg, the poet who had loved her and whom she had given up to marry this bank account man.

With the passionate ardour of adolescence Rebecca had woven an idyll for herself out of her sister's love affair. Felix Weinberg had become for her the symbol of beauty and romance. His voice, his face, the lines he had written to Minnie, coloured Rebecca's longings and dreams. With the love cadence of the poet's voice still stirring in her heart, she put her finger on the door bell.

The door was opened by a trim maid in black, whose superior scrutiny left Rebecca speechless.

Her own sister Minnie with a stiff lady for a servant!

"My sister, is she in? I just came from New York."

"Rebecca!" cried a familiar voice, as she was smothered in hungry arms. "*Oi weh!* How many years! You were yet so little then. Now you're a grown-up person." And overcome by the memories of their ghetto days together, they sobbed in one another's arms.

Rebecca had been prepared for a change in Minnie. Ten years of plenty. But to think that Abe Shmukler with his cloaks and suits could have blotted out the fine sensitiveness of the sister she had loved and left in its place his own gross imprint! Minnie's thin long fingers were now heavy and weighted with diamonds. The slender lines of her figure had grown bulky with fat.

"And to think that you who used to shine up the street like a princess in your home-mades are such a fashion-plate now?" Rebecca laughed reproachfully.

They drew apart and gazed achingly at one another. Rebecca's soul grew faint within her as though her own flesh and blood had grown alien to her. Why couldn't Minnie have lifted Abe to her high thoughts? Why did she let him drag her down to his cloaks and suits—make her a thing of store-bought style?

"Minnie—Minnie!" the younger sister wept, bewildered. "Where have you gone? What have you done with yourself?"

Minnie brushed away her tears and laughed away her sister's reproach. "Did you want me to remain always an East Side *venteh?*"

Then she hugged the young sister with a fresh burst of affection. "Rebecca, you little witch! All you need is a little style. I'll take you to the best stores, and when I get through with you no one will guess that you came from Delancey Street."

"You have the same old heart, Minnie, although you shine like a born Mrs. Vanderbilt."

"No wonder you have no luck for a man with these clothes," Minnie harped back to the thing uppermost in her mind.

"But you weren't fixed up in style when Felix Weinberg was so crazy about you."

"Do you ever see him?" came eagerly.

"Yes, I meet him every once in a while, but his thoughts are far away when he talks to me." She paused, overcome by a rush of feeling. "Sometimes, in my dreams, I feel myself crying out to him, 'Look at me! Can't you see I'm here?'"

"Don't be a little fool and let yourself fall in love with a poet. He's all right for poetry, but to get married you need a man who can make a living. I sent for you not only because I was lonesome and wanted you near, but because I have a man who'll be a great catch for you. He's full of money and crazy to marry himself."

"Aren't there plenty of girls in California for him?"

"But he's like Abe. He wants the plain, settled down kind."

"Am I the plain, settled-down kind like my sister?" thought Rebecca.

And so the whole afternoon sped by in reminiscence of the past and golden plans for the future. Minnie told with pride that her children were sent to a swell camp, where they rubbed sleeves with the millionaires' children of California. Abe had sold out the greater share of his cloaks and suits business to Moe Mirsky—this very man whom Minnie had picked out for Rebecca.

"And if we have the luck to land him, I'll charge you nothing for the matchmaking. My commission will be to have you live near me."

Before Rebecca could answer there was a footstep in the outer hall and a hearty voice called: "So your sister has come! No wonder you're not standing by the door waiting to kiss your husband."

Abe Shmukler, fatter and more prosperous than ten years ago, filled the doorway with his bulk. "Now there'll be peace in the house," he exploded genially. "I've had nothing from my wife but cryings from lonesomeness since I brought her here. You'll have to keep my wife company till we get you a man."

Instinctively Rebecca responded to the fulsomeness of Abe's greeting. His sincerity, his simple joy in welcoming her, touched her. She wondered if her sister had been quite fair to this big, happy-hearted man.

And even as she wondered the vision of Felix Weinberg stood before her. This man of fire and romance and dreams, against Abe Shmukler, was like sunrise and moonrise and song against cloaks and suits. How could any woman who had known the fiery wonder of the poet be content with this tame, ox-like husband?

"I've already picked out a man for you, so you can settle near us for good," said Abe, giving Rebecca another affectionate hug.

Again her heart warmed to him. He was so well intentioned, so lovable. The world needed these plain, bread-and-butter men. Their affection-craving natures, their generous instincts, kept the home fires burning.

Abe fulfilled the great essentials of life. He was a good provider, a good husband, a good father and a genial host. But though he could feed her sister with the fat of the land, what nourishment could this stolid bread-giver provide for the heart, the soul, the mind?

Rebecca's reverie was interrupted by the jangle of the telephone.

"I'll bet it's already that man asking if you arrived." Abe winked at his wife and twitted his sister-in-law under the chin as he picked up the receiver.

"Yes, she's here," Rebecca heard Abe say. And turning to his wife: "Minnie, our friend Moe is coming for dinner."

"Coming right for dinner," cried Minnie. "Quickly we must fix you up. I can't have that man see you looking like a greenhorn just off the ship."

Rebecca surveyed herself critically in the gilt mirror. The excitement of the arrival had brought a faint flush to her cheeks. Her hair had become softer, wavier in the moist California air.

"Why can't I see your Rockefeller prince as I am?" Rebecca was not aware that her charm was enhanced by the very simplicity of her attire. "Is he so high tone that plain me is not good enough for him?"

Her sister cut short her objections and hurried her upstairs, where she tried on one gown after another. But they were all too big.

Then on a sudden thought she snatched a long, fillet scarf, which she draped loosely around Rebecca's neck.

"Why, you look like a picture for a painter." Even Minnie, accustomed now to the last word in style, recognized that the little sister had a charm of personality that needed no store-bought clothes to set it off.

Awaiting them at the foot of the stairs was the smiling Abe. Behind him with one hand grasping the banisters stood a short stocky young man. Under his arm he held tightly to his side a heart-shaped box of candy tied with a flowing red ribbon.

"My, look him over, kid! Ain't he the swellest feller you ever set your eyes on? Ain't you glad you left your ribbon counter for your California prince?"

Moe's colour outshone the red ribbon which tied his box of candy. With a clumsy flourish, he bowed and offered it to the girl. In a panic of confusion, Rebecca let the box slip from her nervous fingers. And Moe stooped jerkily to recover it.

And Abe burst into loud laughter.

"On! Solemiel!" Minnie cried, shaking him by the arm. "You're a grand brother-in-law." And led the way to the dining-room.

Never had Rebecca seen such a rich spread of luxuries. Roast squabs, a silver platter of *gerfulta* fish, shimmering cut glass containing chopped chicken livers and spiced jellies. The under-nourished girl saw for the first time a feast of plenty fit for millionaires.

"What's this—a holiday?" she asked, recovering her voice.

"Don't think you're yet in Delancey Street," admonished the host. "In California the fat of the land is for every day."

As they fell to the food Rebecca understood the over-fed look of those about her. She wondered if she would have sufficient self-control not to make a pig of herself with such delicious plenty, making the eyes glisten, the mouth water, and the heart glad as with song.

Rebecca, watching Moe as he smacked his lips in enjoyment of every mouthful, understood why he wanted the plain, settled-down kind of girl. A home, a wife, and fat dimpling babies belonged to him as flowers and all green-growing things belong to the earth.

"Nu, could you tell on my sister-in-law that she never had meat except on a holiday the way she eats like a bird?" Abe began anew his raillery. And it was not until after dinner, when Minnie dragged her Abe away to a neighbour, that Moe and Rebecca had a chance to talk together.

"I got something grand to show you," Moe burst out once the road was clear. Why waste time and words in the slow love-making of cheap skates who haven't the shekels to show? His money could talk. And he led her out proudly to see his red-lacquered limousine. "Swellest car in the market, and I got it the minute your sister said you were coming."

Rebecca was thrilled with this obvious flattery. It was the first time she had had a man so on his knees to her.

"To-morrow I take you for a ride," he said with the sure tone that came into his voice when he concluded a good sale of cloaks and suits.

She nodded happily as they walked back to the parlour. Moe continued his eager questions. Was she crazy for the movies? Did they have good vaudeville out there on the East Side? Why did she not come sooner to California? His eyes travelled over the girl with thick satisfaction. "How becoming it would be to your diamonds on your neck!" And he rubbed his palms ecstatically.

It was good to be made love to even though the man was not a poet.

Till now she had only eaten out her heart for a look, a word, from Felix Weinberg. What a fool she was not to have come to California a year ago as Minnie had begged her.

"I was so scared I'd be lonesome here, so far away from what I'm used to," she said, with a look that told him that a woman's home is where love is. "Now I wonder how I'll ever be able to go back," she finished softly.

"Go back! You got to stay!" he commanded masterfully. "And I'll see that you shouldn't be so skinny. You got to eat more." And suiting his action to his word, he forced more candy upon the already over-filled girl.

Then he offered to teach her how to play cards. "Minnie and Abe are such grand poker players," he explained.

"My sister Minnie playing cards?"

"Shah! Little queen, you'll have to learn cards, too. There ain't no other pleasure for women here, except cards or the movies or vaudeville, and the bills don't change more than once a week." And he told her that it was the custom in their group to play every night in a different house.

A sudden pity gripped him. He longed to brighten the lonely look of this little greenhorn, put roses into her pale thin cheeks.

"Tell me what is your best pleasure," he asked with the sweeping manner of a Rothschild.

"Ach! How I love music!" The glow of an inner sun lit up her face. "I can't afford a seat in the opera, but even if I have to stand all evening and save the pennies from my mouth, music I've got to have."

"Hah—ha!" He laughed in advance of his own humour. "My sweetest music is the click of the cash register. The ring of the dollars I make is grander to me than the best songs on the phonograph."

His face became suddenly alive. For the first time she saw Moe galvanized into a man of action, a man of power. The light that burned throughout the ages in the eyes of poets and prophets burned also in the eyes of the traders of her race.

"When I was a little hungry boy in the gutters of the ghetto, the only songs I heard were the bargaining cries over pennies. Even when I worked myself up to a clothing store in Division Street they were still tearing my flesh in pieces, squeezing out cheaper, another dime, another nickel from a suit." But the eloquent story of his rise in the world till now—here he was king of clothing—fell upon deaf ears. Rebecca had ceased to listen.

She saw again their kitchen on Sunday night. Felix Weinberg's pale face under the sputtering gas jet, her sister leaning eagerly forward, her hand instinctively reaching towards him across the table, her face alight with the inner radiance that glowed from him like a burning sun. She, Rebecca, close to him, at his feet, all a-tremble with the nearness of him. The children on his knees, clutching at his neck, peering from behind his shoulder. The eternal cadences of Keats and Shelley, the surging rhythm of their song playing upon their hearts, holding them enthralled with a music that they felt all the more deeply because they did not understand.

Even mother, clattering busily with the pots at the stove, would pause in her work, drawn by the magic of the enraptured group.

"*Nu*, with a clean apron I'm also a person to listen," she said as she tore from her the soiled rag which she wore around the stove and reached for a clean blue-checked apron that she wore only for holidays.

"Ah, *Mammeniu!*" Felix would respond. "In honour of this shining beautifulness, I'll read something special for you," and he would, opening his Browning. At the words Rabbi Ben Ezra, *Mammeniu's* sigh was the joy of a child in fairyland.

"Grow old along with me. The best is yet to be,

The last of life for which the first was made."

Then like a child repeating its well-loved lesson for the hundredth time, "*Nu*, I didn't yet live out my years," she would breathe happily. "It will only begin my real life when my children work themselves up in America."

What matter if they had only potato-soup for supper—only the flavour of fried onions in a little suet to take the place of meat? What matter if the only two chairs were patched with boards and the rickety table had for its support a potato barrel? Wonder and beauty filled the room. Voices of poets and prophets of all time were singing in their hearts.

And all that Minnie had given up. For what? For silver platters with *gefulta* fish. For roast squabs. For spiced jellies. And the dollar music from cash registers.

Yes, Minnie, like this blustering Moe, had worked herself up in America. She had a rich house, a Rolls-Royce car, a lady servant to wait on her body. But what had happened to her spirit, her soul—the soul that had once been watered and flowered with the love songs of a poet?

"You see, in California nobody worries for bread," broke in the heavy guttural voice of Moe Mirsky. "People's only trouble is how to enjoy themselves."

Excited, high-pitched voices from the hallway, and Minnie and Abe entered. "So much your sister is crazy for you that she tore herself away from the cards to be with you the first night," said Abe with an inquisitive, quizzical look at the young couple.

"And I was winning at the first shot, too," Minnie added.

"My wife is the best poker player in the bunch," Abe asserted. "Wait, you'll see Friday night when they come around." And turning back to Moe: "You've got to teach her quick the cards so she can join the company."

"Cards don't go in her head at all." Moe looked with unconcealed proprietorship at his future wife. "I guess she ain't yet used to a little pleasure. Let's only introduce her to our society, and she'll soon learn what it is in good time."

The next few days were spent in a wild orgy of shopping. Not only was Rebecca to be made presentable to the higher society in which generous Abe was anxious she should shine, but Minnie was also preparing herself for a month's vacation in Cataline Islands with some of Abe's new real estate friends. As Abe's wife it was a matter of business that she should be more richly dressed than the wives of his prosperous competitors.

For the first time in her life Rebecca saw things bought, not because they were needed, but because they appealed to her sister's insatiable eye.

"When will you ever have enough things?" Rebecca remonstrated. "Why are we going from store to store like a couple of drunkards from bar to bar? The more you buy, the more drunk you get to buy more."

"Just only this one dress. That's the newest thing in style and so becoming."

"But you have so much already. Your closet is so stacked full."

"I saw Mrs. Rosenbaum wear something like it. And Abe wouldn't want she should come dressed better than I."

At last Rebecca was to meet her sister's society friends. Although Minnie and Abe despaired of making little Rebecca stylish, they were satisfied by Friday night that at least she could be introduced without her Delancey Street background too evident.

The dining-room table covered with green baize was piled high with pyramids of poker chips. Packs of cards were on the table. A mahogany cellarette laden with Scotch, cognac, bottles of White Rock and high-ball glasses stood near by.

Minnie was radiant in a black-and-gold spangled dress. The shine of Abe's cheeks outshone the diamond that glistened from his shirt front. Moe, who had arrived before the rest of the guests, had brought Rebecca another heart-shaped gift, containing "the most smelly perfume in the whole drug store."

Before the guests arrived Moe devoted himself to showing Rebecca the sequence of the cards, but try as she would she could make no sense out of it.

"It's such a waste of time. It's so foolish, so brainless...."

"Is it foolish, brainless, to win five hundred, a thousand, in one little night?" cried Moe, the ring of the cash register in his voice.

"It's not only to win money," broke in Minnie. "Cards are life to me. When I play I get so excited I forget about everything. There's no past, no future—only the now, the life of the game."

"Just the same," put in Abe doggedly. "When you win you're crazy to grab in more, and when you lose you're crazy to stake it all to win again."

Dimly Rebecca began to see the lure of gambling. It was as contagious as small-pox. Minnie had caught the poison from Abe and his friends. In a world where there was no music, no books, no spiritual stimulus, where people had nothing but money, what else was there to fill the eternal emptiness but excitement?

The guests arrived. Mrs. Rosenbaum and her husband, the biggest department store owner of Los Angeles. Mr. and Mrs. Soikolsky, real estate owners of half of Hollywood. Mr. Einstein, the Tecla of California, whose wife and children had just sailed for the Orient.

As Rebecca was introduced to one solid citizen after another, she was unable to distinguish between them. The repellently prosperous look of the "all-rightnik" stamped them all. The vulgar boastfulness of the man who had forced his way up in the world only to look down with smug superiority upon his own people.

"Always with your thoughts in the air," chuckled Moe, a stubby hand tenderly reaching towards her.

The sad eyes of the little greenhorn stirred vague memories in his heart. Warming things welled up in him to say to her. But Abe interrupted by calling the guests to their places.

A wave of expectancy swept over the gathering as they elbowed themselves about the table. Eyes sharp. Measuring glances shot from one to the other. A business-like air settled upon the group.

Abe poured a generous drink of whisky for each. "*Nu*, my friends, only get yourself drunk enough so I can have a chance to win once from you."

A fresh pack of cards was opened. The deal fell to the tight-laced, high-bosomed Mrs. Rosenbaum, whose fat fingers flashed with diamonds as she dealt.

"You got to sit here, by me, all evening to bring me luck," Moe whispered in Rebecca's ear, and drew a chair for her alongside of him.

An audible silence pervaded the room. The serious business of the game began.

Unconsciously Rebecca was caught by the contagion of their excitement. She even began to hope that Minnie would win, that she would bring luck to the well-meaning Moe.

"Usual limit five dollars," Abe declared.

Moe explained that the white chips represented one dollar, the blue two, the red five, and the yellow ten.

Slowly the air became filled with smoke and the smell of alcohol. The betting rose higher and higher. Rebecca could stand it no longer and rushed from the room to the parlour. She looked with sharp distaste at the gaudy furnishings. Till now she had been taken in by the glamour of her sister's wealth. But now the crowded riches of the place choked her. Who had chosen all this? Her sister or her sister's husband? Here and there was a beautiful pillow or finely woven rug, but its beauty was killed by the loud clash of colour, the harsh glare of cheap gilt. Cheapness and showiness stuck like varnish over the costly fabrics of the room. It was a sort of furniture display Rebecca had often seen in department stores. It smelled cloaks and suits.

The vivid pale face of the poet, with eyes that burned with the fire of beauty, gazed accusingly at the rich velvet hangings and overstuffed furniture that had won Minnie away from him.

How different Minnie's home would have been if she had married the poet! A small room in a tenement. A bare floor. A bare table. A room that lacked beautiful things but was filled with beautiful thoughts. Felix Weinberg's flaming presence, the books he read, the dreams he dreamed, the high thoughts that lit up his face would have filled the poorest room with sunshine.

The shrill voices of the dining-room startled her.

"Ach! What's the matter?" Rebecca gasped in a panic. "Are they killing themselves?" and hurried in.

She could hardly distinguish the faces, so thick was the air with smoke and whisky fumes. The look of wild animals distorted their features. Mrs. Rosenbaum's hair had slipped from its net. Her own sister was flushed, dishevelled. Moe's face was set in sullen, bitter lines as he called for more money. A scoffing devil of greed seemed to possess them all. It was Bedlam let loose.

"No use showing that you come from Division Street, even if you did lose a couple of hundred," Minnie shrilled savagely at Moe.

"You're worse than that push-cart, Kike," leered the half-drunken Abe. "What a wife! What a wife! She'd steal the whites out from my eyes. She'd grab the gold out of my teeth."

There followed an avalanche of abuse between her sister, her husband and the sodden Moe. Rebecca had never heard such language used.

"They're only drunk. They don't know what they're saying," she apologized for them herself.

Thank God, her mother, her father couldn't see what cloaks and suits had made of Minnie. Her own sister a common card-player! Where was that gentle bud of a girl that Felix had loved? How was that fine spirit of hers lost in this wild lust for excitement? And these people whom she called friends, this very Moe whom she had picked out for her to marry—what were they? All-rightniks—the curse of their people, the shame of their race, Jews dehumanized, destroyed by their riches. Glutted stomachs—starved souls, escaped from the prison of poverty to smother themselves in the fleshpots of plenty.

It was towards noon the next day that Minnie with dull, puffy eyes and aching head stumbled into Rebecca's room. The half-filled valise was on the bed, clothes were piled on chairs, and the trunk open as though ready for packing.

"What's this? Are you eloping with Moe?" Minnie was too spent from the night of excitement to be surprised at anything, but a closer look at Rebecca's tear-stained face aroused her from her apathy. "*Yok!* Can't you speak?" she demanded irritably.

"My God! How can you stand it here—this life of the flesh? What have you here, in this land of plenty, but overeating, oversleeping——"

"Why shouldn't I over-eat?" Minnie hurled back. "I was starved enough all my youth. Never knew the taste of meat or milk till I came here. I slaved long enough in the sweat-shop. The world owes me a little rest." Her face grew hard with bitter memories. "I don't know how I stood it there, in the dirt of Delancey Street, ten people in three rooms, like herrings in a barrel, without a bath-tub, without——"

"Marble bath-tubs—bathing yourself morning and night don't yet keep your soul alive. How could you have sunk yourself into such drunken card-playing?"

"If not for cards I'd be dead from loneliness. Are there any people to talk to here?" She threw out bediamonded hands in a gesture of helplessness. "I hate Abe like poison when he's home so much of the time. Cards and clothes help me run away from myself—help me forget my terrible emptiness." Minnie reached out imploringly to her sister. "Here you see how I'm dying before your eyes, and yet you want to leave me."

Rebecca felt herself growing hard and inhuman. Didn't she love her sister enough to respond to her cry of loneliness? But the next moment she knew that though it tore the heart out of her body she could never stand this bloated ease of the flesh into which Minnie was trying to beguile her.

"Would you want me to marry Moe and bury myself alive in cloaks and suits like you? I'd rather starve on dry crusts where life is real, where there's still hope for higher things. It would kill me to stay here another day. Your fine food, your fresh air, your velvet limousine smothers me.... It's all a desert of emptiness painted over with money. Nothing is real. The sky is too blue. The grass is too green. This beauty is all false paint, hiding dry rot. There's only one hope for you. Leave your killing comforts and come with me."

"And what about the children?" Minnie leaped to her feet in quick defence. "I want them to have a chance in life. I couldn't bear to have them go through the misery and dirt that nearly killed me. You're not a mother. You don't know a mother's heart."

"Your mother's heart—it's only selfishness! You're only trying to save yourself the pain of seeing your children go through the struggle that made you what you are. No," she corrected, "that made you what you once were."

Rebecca towered over her sister like the living spirit of struggle revolting against the deadening inertia of ease.

"What is this chance that you are giving your children? To rub sleeves with millionaire children? Will that feed their hungry young hearts? Fire their spirits for higher things? Children's hands reach out for struggle. Their youth is hungry for hardships, for danger, for the rough fight with life even more than their bodies are hungry for bread."

Minnie looked at her little sister. From where came that fire, that passion? She saw again Felix Weinberg's flaming eyes. She heard again his biting truths, the very cadence of his voice.

Minnie buried her throbbing head in the pillows. As surely as Rebecca sold ribbons over the counter at ten cents a yard, so surely Minnie knew that she had sold her own soul for the luxuries which Abe's money had bought. And now it was out of her power to call this real part of her back. The virus of luxury had eaten into her body and soul till she could no longer exist without it.

"If I could only go back with you," she sobbed impotently, "if I could only go back."

Love and hate tore at Rebecca's heart—love of Minnie and hatred of the fleshpots that were destroying her sister. The days and nights of journey home were spent in tortured groping for the light. Ach—sisters! Flesh of one flesh, blood of one blood, aching to help one another in the loneliness of life, yet doomed like strangers to meet only to part again.

If she could only talk out her confusion to someone. Felix Weinberg! How he could make her clear! And suddenly she knew—knew with burning certainty that after ten years of worshipping him at a distance she must come to him face to face. Truth itself was driving her to him.

As she got off the train, her feet instinctively led her to the cellar café on East Broadway, where far into the morning hours Felix Weinberg and his high-thinking friends were to be found.

Even before she caught sight of him at a corner table surrounded by his followers, she felt a vast release. She looked in through the grated window. How different these—her own people—from the dollar-chasers she had just left! The dirt, the very squalor of the place was life to her, as the arrogant cleanliness, the strutting shirt-fronts of cloaks and suits had deadened her. Here rags talked high thoughts and world philosophies, like princes at a royal court. Here only what was in your heart and head counted, not your bank account or the shine of your diamonds.

Even the torn wall-plaster in this palace of dreams had a magic all its own. The pictures, the poems, the fragmentary bits of self-expression that were scribbled everywhere were marks of the vivid life that surged about—clamouring to be heard.

She never knew how she got inside, but as in a dream she heard herself talking to *him*—looking straight into Felix's eyes in a miraculously natural way as though her whole life was but a leading up to this grand moment.

The youth who used to light up their little kitchen with his flaming presence was gone. In his place had come a man grown strong with suffering. Fine as silk and strong as steel shone every feature. He was scarred with all the hurts of the world—hurts that lay like whip lashes on the furrows of his face. She felt nothing would be too small or too big for him to understand.

"Years ago when I was only that big at your feet," Rebecca measured the table height with her hand, "your words were life to me. Now I come three thousand miles to talk my heart out with you." And she told him everything, her doubt of herself, her hard intolerance of the plain bread-and-butter people, her revolt against her own flesh and blood.

His face lit with quick comprehension. He stopped sipping his glass of tea and leaned towards her across the table. With every word, with every gesture she revealed herself as one of his own kind! This girl of whose existence he had scarcely been aware all these years seemed suddenly to have grown up under his very eyes, and he had not seen her till now.

"Don't you see, little heart," he responded warmly, "the dollars are their dreams. They eat the fleshpots with the same passionate intensity that they once fasted in faith on the Day of Atonement. They've been hungry for so many centuries. Let them eat! Give them only a chance for a few generations. They'll find their souls again. The deeper down under the surface you get, the more you see that the dollar-chasers are also pursuing a dream, but their dream is different from ours, that is all."

"Where did you get to feel and know so much?" she breathed adoringly.

He did not answer. But his eyes dwelt on her in ardent reverie, marvelling at the gift of the gods that she was. Through unceasing frustration of the things for which he had striven, he had come to a point of understanding the materialists no less than the dreamers. He had learned to forgive even Minnie who had turned from his love for the security of wealth. But here was the glowing innocence of a girl with the heart and brain of a woman—a woman in his own poet's world, one who had rejected the fleshpots of her own free will. It was as though after years of parching thirst life had suddenly brought him a draught of wine, a heady vintage of youth, of living poetry, of love perhaps. Straining closer to her, he abandoned himself to the exaltation that swept him and kissed her hand.

"No—no! It was Minnie you always loved," Rebecca gasped, frightened at his ardour.

"Minnie I loved as a dreaming youth, a half-fledged poet," he flashed back at her. "But you—you——"

She knew now why she had come back home again—back to the naked struggle for bread—back to the crooked, narrow streets filled with shouting children, the haggling push-carts and bargaining housewives—back to the relentless, penny-pinched poverty—but a poverty rich in romance, in dreams—rich in its very hunger of unuttered, unsung beauty.

THE SONG TRIUMPHANT

The Story of Beret Pinsky, Poet of the People, who Sold his Soul for Wealth

§ 1

"Where went your week's wages?" demanded Hanneh Breineh, her bony back humping like an angry cat's as she bent over the washtub.

Terrified, Moisheh gazed wildly at the ceiling, then dropped his eyes to the floor.

"Your whole week's wages—where went it?" insisted Hanneh.

She turned from the tub and brandished her hands in his face.

"The shoes—Berel's shoes," Moisheh stumblingly explained. "I—I had to buy him shoes for his feet—not new shoes—only second-hand."

"Shoes yet for such a loafer? I'd drive him out naked—barefoot. Let him get the chills—the fever—only to get rid from him quick!"

None of the roomers of Hanneh Breineh's lodging-house could escape her tyrannous inquisition. Had she not been a second mother to Moisheh, the pants presser, and to Berel, his younger brother? Did she not cook their supper for them every night, without any extra charge? In return for this motherly service she demanded a precise account of their expenditures of money or time, and of every little personal detail of their lives.

Red glints shot from Hanneh Breineh's sunken eyes.

"And for what more did you waste out my rent money?"

"Books—he got to have 'em—more'n eating—more'n life!"

"Got to have books?" she shrieked. "Beggars—*schnorrers*—their rent not paid—their clothes falling from them in rags—and yet they buy themselves books!" Viciously slapping the board with the shirt she had been rubbing, she straightened and faced Moisheh menacingly. "I been too good to you. I cooked and washed for you, and killed myself away to help you for nothing. So that's my thanks!"

The door opened. A lean youth with shining eyes and a dishevelled mass of black hair rushed in.

"*Ach*, Moisheh! Already back from the shop? My good luck—I'm choking to tell you!"

The two drab figures huddled in the dim kitchen between the washtub and the stove gazed speechless at the boy. Even Hanneh Breineh was galvanized for the moment by the ecstatic, guileless face, the erect, live figure poised bird-like with desire.

"*Oi*, golden heart!" The boy grasped Moisheh's arm impetuously. "A typewriter! It's worth fifty dollars—maybe more yet—and I can get it for ten, if I grab it quick for cash!"

Moisheh glanced from the glowering landlady to his ardent brother. His gentle heart sank as he looked into Berel's face, with its undoubting confidence that so reasonable a want would not be denied him.

"Don't you think—maybe—ain't there something you could do to earn the money?"

"What more can I do than I'm already doing? You think only pressing pants is work?"

"Berel," said Moisheh, with frank downrightness, "you got your education. Why don't you take up a night school? They're looking for teachers."

"Me a teacher? Me in that treadmill of deadness? Why, the dullest hand in a shop got more chance to use his brains than a teacher in their schools!"

"Well, then, go to work in a shop—only half-days—the rest of the time give yourself over to your dreams in the air."

"Brother, are you gone crazy?" Berel gesticulated wildly. "I should go into that terrible sweat and grind of the machines? All the fire that creates in me would die in a day!"

The poet looked at the toil-scarred face of his peasant brother. For all his crude attempts at sympathy, how could he, with the stink of steam soaked into his clothes, with his poverty-crushed, sweatshop mind—how could he understand the anguish of thwarted creation, of high-hearted hopes that died unvoiced?

"But everybody got to work," Moisheh went on. "All your poetry is grand, but it don't pay nothing."

"Is my heart cry nothing, then? Nothing to struggle by day and by night for the right word in this strange English, till I bleed away from the torture of thoughts that can't come out?"

Berel stopped, and his eyes seemed transfigured with an inner light. His voice grew low and tense. Each word came deliberately, with the precision he used when swayed by poetic feeling.

"*Ach*, if I could only tell you of the visions that come to me! They flash like burning rockets over the city by night. Lips, eyes, a smile—they whisper to me a thousand secrets. The feelings that leap in my heart are like rainbow-coloured playthings. I toss them and wrestle with them; and yet I must harness them. Only then can they utter the truth, when they are clear and simple so that a young child could understand."

Turning swiftly, the words hissed from the poet's lips.

"Why do I have to bite the dirt for every little crumb you give me? I, who give my life, the beat of my heart, the blood of my veins, to bring beauty into the world—why do I have to beg—beg!"

He buried his face in his hands, utterly overcome.

Moisheh, with an accusing glance at Hanneh Breineh, as if she was in some measure to blame for this painful outburst, soothed the trembling Berel as one would a child.

"*Shah!*" He took from his pocket all his money. "Two dollars is all I yet got left, and on this I must stick out till my wages next Monday. But here, Berel, take half."

Shamed by Moisheh's generosity, and embittered by the inadequacy of the sum, Berel's mood of passionate pleading gave way to sullenness.

"Keep it!" he flung over his shoulder, and left the room.

§ 2

Berel's thoughts surged wildly as he raced through the streets.

"Why am I damned and despised by them all? What is my crime? That I can't compromise? That I fight with the last breath to do my work—the work for which I was born?"

Instinctively his feet led him to the public library, his one sanctuary of escape from the sordidness of the world. But now there seemed no peace for him even here.

"Money—money!" kept pounding and hammering in his ears. "Get money or be blotted out!"

A tap on his shoulder. Berel turned and looked into a genial face, sleeked and barbered into the latest mould of fashion.

"Jake Shapiro!" cried the poet.

Five years ago these two had met on the ship bound for America. What dreams they had dreamed together on that voyage—Berel Pinsky, the poet, and Shapiro, the musician!

"What are you doing for a living? Still writing poetry?" asked Shapiro, as he glanced appraisingly at the haggard-eyed youth. In one swift look he took in the shabby garments that covered the thin body, the pride and the eagerness of the pale, hungry face. "I guess," added the musician, "your poetry ain't a very paying proposition!"

Incensed at the unconscious gibe, Berel turned with a supercilious curl of his lips.

"What's a sport like you doing here in the library?"

Shapiro pointed to a big pile of books from the copyright office.

"Chasing song titles," he said. "I'm a melody writer. I got some wonderful tunes, and I thought I'd get a suggestion for a theme from these catalogues."

"*Oi weh*, if for ideas you have to go to copyright catalogues!"

"Man, you should see the bunch of lyric plumbers I have to work with. They give me jingles and rhymes, but nothing with a real heart thrill." He turned on Berel with sudden interest. "Show us some of your soul stuff."

Berel handed several pages to the composer. One after another, Shapiro read.

"Highbrow—over the heads of the crowd," was his invariable comment.

Suddenly he stopped.

"By heck, there's a good idea for a sob song! What a title—'Aching Hearts'!" He grasped Berel's hand with genuine friendliness. "Your lines have the swing I've been looking for. Only a little more zip, a change here and there, and——"

"Change this?" Berel snatched the verses and put them back in his pocket. "There's my heart's blood in every letter of it!"

"Yes, it's heart stuff all right," placated the composer, realizing a good thing, and impatient as a hound on the scent. "Come along!" He took Berel by the arm. "I want to read your sob stuff to a little friend."

Flattered, but vaguely apprehensive, Berel followed Shapiro to the delectable locality known as Tin Pan Alley, and into the inner shrine of one of the many song houses to be found there.

"Maizie!" cried Shapiro to a vaudeville star who had been waiting none too patiently for his return. "I've found an honest-to-God poet!"

He introduced Berel, who blushed like a shy young girl.

"So you're a poet?" said Maizie.

Her eyes were pools of dancing lights as she laughed, aware of her effect on the transfixed youth. Berel stared in dazzled wonder at the sudden apparition of loveliness, of joy, of life. Soft, feminine perfume enveloped his senses. Like a narcotic, it stole over him. It was the first time he had ever been touched by the seductive lure of woman.

Shapiro sat down at a piano, and his hands brought from the tortured instrument a smashing medley of syncopated tunes.

"This needs lyric stuff with a heartbeat in it," he flung over his shoulder; "and you have just the dope."

His eyes met Maizie's significantly, and then veered almost imperceptibly in the direction of Berel.

"Go ahead, kid—vamp him! We've got to have him," was the message they conveyed to her.

Maizie put her hand prettily on the youth's arm.

"With an air like that, and the right lines—oh, boy, I'd flood Broadway with tears!"

Berel stood bewildered under the spell of her showy beauty. Unconsciously his hand went to his pocket, where lay his precious verses.

"I—I can't change my lines for the mob," he stammered.

But Maizie's little hand crept down his arm until it, too, reached his pocket, while her face was raised alluringly to his.

"Let's see it, Mr. Poet—do, please!"

Suddenly, with a triumphant ripple of laughter, she snatched the pages and glanced rapidly through the song. Then, with her highly manicured fingers, she grasped the lapels of Berel's coat, her eyes dancing with a coquettish little twinkle.

"It's wonderful!" she flattered. "Just give me the chance to put it over, and all the skirts from here to Denver will be singing it!"

Shapiro placed himself in front of Berel and said with businesslike directness:

"I'll advance you two hundred bucks on this song, if you'll put a kick in it."

Two hundred dollars! The suddenness of the overwhelming offer left Berel stunned and speechless.

"Money—*ach*, money! To get a breath of release from want!" he thought. "Just a few weeks away from Hanneh Breineh's cursing and swearing! A chance to be quiet and alone—a place where I can have a little beauty!"

Shapiro, through narrowed lids, watched the struggle that was going on in the boy. He called for his secretary.

"Write out a contract," he ordered. "Words by Berel Pinsky—my melody."

Then he turned to the poet, who stood nervously biting his lips.

"If this song goes over, it'll mean a big piece of change for you. You get a cent and a half on every copy. A hit sometimes goes a million copies. Figure it out for yourself. I'm not counting the mechanical end of it—phonograph records—pianola rolls—hurdy-gurdies."

At the word "hurdy-gurdy" an aching fear shot through the poet's heart. His pale face grew paler as he met the smooth smile of the composer.

"Only to get a start," he told himself, strengthening his resolve to sell his poem with an equal resolve never to do so again.

"Well?" chuckled Shapiro.

He drew out a thick wallet from his pocket, and began counting out the fresh, green bills.

"I'll do it this once," said Berel, in a scarcely audible voice, as he pocketed the money.

"Gassed with gold!" exulted Shapiro to Maizie after Berel left. "He's ours body and soul—bought and paid for!"

§ 3

Hanneh Breineh's lodging-house was in a hubbub of excitement. A limousine had stopped before the dingy tenement, and Berel—a Berel from another world—stepped into the crowded kitchen.

How he was dressed! His suit was of the latest cut. The very quality of his necktie told of the last word in grooming. The ebony cane hanging on his arm raised him in the eyes of the admiring boarders to undreamed-of heights of wealth.

There was a new look in his eyes—the look of the man who has arrived and who knows that he has. Gone was the gloom of the insulted and the injured. Success had blotted out the ethereal, longing gaze of the hungry ghetto youth. Nevertheless, to a discerning eye, a lurking discontent, like a ghost at a feast, still cast its shadow on Berel's face.

"He's not happy. He's only putting on," thought Moisheh, casting sidelong glances at his brother.

"You got enough to eat, and it shows on you so quick," purred Hanneh Breineh, awed into ingratiating gentleness by Berel's new prosperity.

With a large-hearted gesture, Berel threw a handful of change into the air for the children. There was a wild scramble of tangled legs and arms, and then a rush to the street for the nearest pushcart.

"Oi weh!" Hanneh Breineh touched Berel with reverent gratitude. "Give a look only how he throws himself around with his money!"

Berel laughed gleefully, a warm glow coming to his heart at this bubbling appreciation of his generosity.

"Hanneh Breineh," he said, with an impressive note in his voice, "did you ever have a twenty-dollar gold piece in your hand?"

An intake of breath was the only answer.

"Here it is."

Berel took from his pocket a little satin case and handed it to her, his face beaming with the lavishness of the gift.

Hanneh Breineh gazed at the gold piece, which glistened with unbelievable solidity before her enraptured eyes. Then she fell on Berel's neck.

"You diamond prince!" she gushed. "Always I stood for your part when they all said you was crazy!"

The lean, hungry-faced boarders drank him in, envious worship in their eyes.

"Rockefeller—Vanderbilt!"

Exclamations of wonder and awe leaped from lip to lip as they gazed at this Midas who was once a *schnorrer* in their midst.

Basking in their adulation like a bright lizard in the sun, Berel, with feigned indifference, lighted a thick cigar. He began to hum airily one of his latest successes.

"Ten thousand dollars for my last song!" he announced casually, as he puffed big rings of smoke to the ceiling.

"Riches rains on you!" Hanneh Breineh threw up her hands in an abandon of amazement. "Sing to me only that millionaires' song!"

Lifting her ragged skirts, she began to step in time to the tune that Berel hummed.

Out of all the acclaimers Moisheh remained the only unresponsive figure in the room.

"Why your long face?" Hanneh Breineh shrieked. "What thunder fell on you?"

Moisheh shifted uncomfortably.

"I don't know what is with me the matter. I don't get no feelings from the words. It's only boom—boom—nothing!"

"Is ten thousand dollars nothing?" demanded the outraged Hanneh Breineh. "Are a million people crazy? All America sings his songs, and you turn up your nose on them. What do you know from life? You sweat from morning till night pressing out your heart's blood on your ironing board, and what do you get from it? A crooked back—a dried out herring face!"

"'The prosperity of fools slayeth them,'" quoted Moisheh in Hebrew.

Berel turned swiftly on his brother.

"It's the poets who are slain and the fools who are exalted. Before I used to spend three months polishing one little cry from the heart. Sometimes I sold it for five dollars, but most of the time I didn't. Now I shoot out a song in a day, and it nets me a fortune!"

"But I would better give you the blood from under my nails than you should sell yourself for dollars," replied Moisheh.

"Would you want me to come back to this hell of dirt and beg from you again for every galling bite of bread?" cried Berel, flaring into rage. "Your gall should burst, you dirt-eating muzhik!" he shouted with unreasoning fury, and fled headlong from the room.

This unaccountable anger from the new millionaire left all but Hanneh Breineh in a stupor of bewilderment.

"Muzhik! Are we all muzhiks, then?" she cried. A biting doubt of the generosity of her diamond prince rushed through her. "Twenty dollars only from so many thousands? What if he did dress out his stingy present in a satin box?"

She passed the gold piece around disdainfully.

"After all, I can't live on the shine from it. What'll it buy me—only twenty dollars? I done enough for him when he was a starving beggar that he shouldn't be such a piker to me!"

§ 4

A night of carousing had just ended. Berel Pinsky looked about his studio. Wineglasses were strewn about. Hairpins and cigarette ashes littered the floor. A woman's rainbow-coloured scarf, reeking with tobacco smoke and perfume, lay wantonly across the piano keys.

He strode to the window and raised the shade, but quickly pulled it down again. The sunlight hurt him. The innocent freshness of the morning blew accusingly against his hot brow.

He threw himself on the couch, but he could not rest. Like a distorted mirror, his mind reflected the happenings of the night before.

A table decked with flowers and glittering with silver and glass swam in vinous streaks of purple and amber. Berel saw white shoulders and sinuous arms—women's soft flesh against the black background of men's dress coats.

One mocking moment rose out of the reeling picture. A bright head pressed against his breast. His arms encircled a slender silken body. Pinnacled high above the devouring faces of his guests, hectic verses sputtered from his lips with automatic fluency.

It was this scene, spurting out of his blurred vision, that stabbed him like a hidden enemy within his soul. He had prostituted the divine in him for the swinish applause of the mob!

"God help me! God help me!" His body swayed back and forth in dumb, driven helplessness. "My sin!" he moaned, and sank to his knees.

Unconsciously he recalled the ritual chant of the Hebrews on the Day of Atonement—a chant he had not heard since he was a little child in Russia.

"'My sin—the sin I committed wilfully and the sin without will. Behold, I am like a vessel filled with shame and confusion!'"

As he repeated the chant, beating his breast, his heart began to swell and heave with the old racial hunger for purging, for cleanness.

"My sin!" he cried. "I took my virgin gift of song and dragged it through the mud of Broadway!"

His turbulent penance burst into sobs—broke through the parched waste within him. From afar off a phrase fragrant as dew, but vague and formless, trembled before him. With a surge of joy, he seized pencil and paper. Only to catch and voice the first gush of his returning spirit!

"Wake up, you nut!"

Shapiro had come in unobserved, and stood before him like a grinning Mephistopheles. Berel looked up, startled. The air boiled before him.

"See here—we got the chance of our life!" Shapiro, in his enthusiasm, did not notice Berel's grim mood. He shook the poet by the shoulder. "Ten thousand bucks, and not a worry in your bean! Just sign your name to this."

With a shudder of shame, Berel glanced at the manuscript and flung it from him.

"Sign my name to this trash?"

"Huh! You're mighty squeamish all of a sudden!"

"I can't choke no more my conscience."

"Conscience, rot! If we can't get the dope from you, I tell you, we got to get it from somebody else till you get back on the job!"

A cloud seemed to thicken Berel's glance.

"Here," he said, taking from his desk his last typewritten songs, "I've done my level best to grind this out."

Shapiro grasped the sheets with quickening interest. He read, and then shook his head with grieved finality.

"It's no use. It's not in you any more. You've lost the punch."

"You mean to tell me that my verses wouldn't go?"

Berel's eyes shone like hot coals out of his blanched face.

"Look here, old pal," replied Shapiro, with patronizing pity. "You've just gone dry."

"You ghoul!" Berel lifted his fist threateningly. "It's you who worked me dry—made of my name nothing but a trade-mark!"

"So that's what I get for all I done for you!" Revulsion at the boy's ingratitude swept through Shapiro like a fury. "What do you think I am? Business is business. If you ain't got the dope no more, why, you ain't better than the bunch of plumbers that I chucked!"

With a guttural cry, Berel hurled himself forward like a tiger.

"You bloodsucker, you!"

A shriek from Maizie standing in the doorway. A whirling figure in chiffon and furs thrust itself between them, the impact pushing Shapiro back.

"Baby darling, you're killing me!" Soft arms clung about Berel's neck. "You don't want to hurt nobody—you know you don't—and you make me cry!"

Savagely Berel thrust the girl's head back and looked into her eyes. His face flashed with the shame of the betrayed manhood in him.

"I was a poet before you smothered my fire with your jazz!"

For an instant Maizie's features froze, terrified by an anger that she could not comprehend. Then she threw herself on his shoulder again.

"But it's in rehearsal—booked to the coast. It's all up with me unless you sign!"

He felt her sobs pounding away his anger. A hated tenderness slowly displaced his fury. Unwillingly, his arms clasped her closer.

"This once, but never again," he breathed in her ear as he crushed her to him.

Gently Maizie extricated herself, with a smile shining through her tear-daubed face.

"You darling old pet! I'll be grateful till I die," she said, thrusting the pen into Berel's hand.

With tragic acceptance of his weakness, Berel scrawled his well-known signature on one sheet after another. With a beaten look of hatred he handed them to Shapiro, now pacified and smiling.

Long after they had gone, Berel still sat in the same chair. He made no move. He uttered no sound. With doubled fists thrust between his knees, he sat there, his head sunk on his breast.

In the depths of his anguish a sudden light flashed. He picked up the rejected songs and read them with regained understanding. All the cheap triteness, the jazz vulgarity of the lines, leaped at him and hit him in the face.

"Pfui!" he laughed with bitter loathing, as he flung the tawdry verses from him.

Like a prisoner unbound, he sprang to his feet. He would shake himself free from the shackles of his riches! All this clutter of things about him—this huge, stuffy house with its useless rooms—the servants—his limousine—each added luxury was only another bar shutting him out from the light.

For an instant he pondered how to get rid of his stifling wealth. Should he leave it to Moisheh or Hanneh Breineh? No—they should not be choked under this mantle of treasure that had nearly choked the life in him.

A flash of inspiration—Maizie! God help her, poor life-loving Maizie! He would give it to her outright—everything, down to the last kitchen pot—only to be a free man again!

As quick as thought Berel scribbled a note to his lawyer, directing him to carry out this reckless whim. Then he went to the closet where, out of some strange, whimsical sentiment, he still kept his shabby old coat and hat. In a moment he was the old Berel again. Still in his frenzy, he strode towards the door.

"Back—back to Hanneh Breineh—to Moisheh—back to my own people! Free—free!"

He waved his hands exultantly. The walls resounded with his triumphant laughter. Grasping his shabby old cap in his hand, he raised it high over his head and slammed the gold-panelled door behind him with a thundering crash.

§ 5

"Last lot cheap! Apples sweet like honey!"

"Fish, live, fresh fish!"

"Shoe laces, matches, pins!"

The raucous orchestra of voices rose and fell in whining, blatant discord. Into the myriad sounds the rumbling Elevated bored its roaring thunder. Dirty, multi-coloured rags—the pinions of poverty—fluttered from the crowded windows. Streams of human atoms surged up and down the side-walk littered with filth. Horses and humans pounded and scuttled through the middle of the street.

Berel's face shone exultant out of the crowd. In the quickening warmth of this old, familiar poverty his being expanded and breathed in huge drafts of air. The jostling mass of humanity that pressed about him was like the close embrace of countless friends.

Ach, here in this elemental struggle for existence was the reality he was seeking! It cried to him out of the dirty, driven faces. Here was the life that has never yet been fully lived. Here were the songs that have not yet been adequately sung.

"A black year on you, robber, swindler! If I go to buy rotten apples, should you charge me for fruit from heaven?"

The familiar voice shot like a bolt to his awakening heart. He looked up to see Hanneh Breineh's ragged figure wedged in between two pushcarts, her face ecstatic with the zest of bargaining.

"Hanneh Breineh!" he cried, seizing her market basket, and almost throwing himself on her neck in a rush of exuberant affection. "I've come back to you and Moisheh!"

"God from the world! What's this—you in rags?" A quick look of suspicion crept into her face. "Did you lose your money? Did you maybe play cards?"

"I left it all to her—you know—every cent of the ill-gotten money."

"Left your money to that doll's face?"

Hanneh clutched her head and peered at him out of her red-lidded eyes.

"Where's Moisheh?" Berel asked.

He came closer to her, his whole face expressing the most childlike faith in her acceptance of his helplessness, in the assurance of her welcome.

"Don't you yet know the pants pressers was on a strike, and he owed me the rent for so long he went away from shame?"

"But where is he—my brother?" cried Berel in despair.

"The devil knows, not me. I only know he owes me the rent!"

"Moisheh gone?" He felt the earth slipping from under him. He seized Hanneh Breineh's hand imploringly. "You can squeeze me in with the other boarders—put me up on chairs—over the washtub—anywhere. I got no one but you!"

"No one but me?" Thrusting him down to his knees, she towered above him like some serpent-headed fury. "What did you ever done for me when you had it good that I should take pity on you now? Why was you such a stingy to me when you were rolling yourself in riches?"

Her voice came in thick gusts of passion, as the smouldering feeling of past neglect burst from her in volcanic wrath. "You black-hearted *schnorrer*, you!"

A crowd of neighbours and passers-by, who had gathered at her first cursing screams, now surged closer. With her passion for harangue, she was lifted to sublime heights of vituperative eloquence by her sensation-hungry audience.

"People! Give a look only! This soft idiot throws away all his money on a doll's face, and then wants me to take the bread from the mouths of my own children to feed him!" She shook her fist in Berel's face. "Loafer—liar! I was always telling you your bad end!"

A hoarse voice rose from the crowd.

"Pfui! the rotten rich one!"

"He used to blow from himself like a Vanderbilt!"

"Came riding around in automobiles!"

All the pent-up envy that they never dared express while he was in power suddenly found voice.

"He's crazy—*meshugeh!*"

The mob took up the abuse and began to press closer. A thick piece of mud from an unknown hand flattened itself on the ashen cheek of the shaken poet. Instantly the lust for persecution swept the crowd. Mud rained on the crouching figure in their midst. Hoarse invectives, shrieks, infamous laughter rose from the mob, now losing all control.

With the look of a hunted beast, Berel drove his way through the merciless crowd. His clothing swirled in streaming rags behind him as he fled on, driven by the one instinct to escape alive.

When he had outdistanced those who pursued, he dropped in a dark hallway of an alley. Utter exhaustion drained him of all thought, all feeling.

Dawn came. Still Berel slept. From the near-by street the clattering of a morning milk wagon roused him slightly. He stirred painfully, then sank back into a dream which grew as vivid as life.

He saw himself a tiny, black ant in an ant-hill. While plodding toilfully with the teeming hive, he suddenly ventured on a path of his own. Then a huge, destroying force overwhelmed and crushed him, to the applause of the other ants, slaves of their traditional routine.

The pounding of a hammer rang above his head. He opened his eyes. A man was nailing a sign to the doorway into which he had sunk the night before. Berel rubbed his heavy-lidded eyes and, blinking, read the words:

MACHINE HANDS WANTED

"Food! *Oi weh*, a bite to eat! A job should I take?"

The disjointed thoughts of his tired brain urged him to move. He tried to rise, but he ached in every limb. The pain in his stiff body brought back to him the terror through which he had lived the day before. More than starvation, he feared the abyss of madness that yawned before him.

"Machine hand—anything," he told himself. "Only to be sane—only to be like the rest—only to have peace!"

This new humility gave him strength. He mounted the stairs of the factory and took his place in the waiting line of applicants for work.

§ 6

For weeks Berel Pinsky worked, dull and inanimate as the machines he had learned to drive. Work, eat, sleep—eat, sleep, work. Day after day he went to and from his hall bedroom, day after day to and from the shop.

He had ceased to struggle. He had ceased to be an individual, a soul apart. He was a piece of a mass, a cog of a machine, an ant of an ant hill. Individually he was nothing—they were nothing. Together they made up the shop.

So he went on. Inert, dumb as a beast in a yoke, he brushed against his neighbours. He never talked. As if in a dream, he heard the shrill babble of the other shop hands rise above the roaring noises of the machines.

One day, while eating his scanty lunch, lost in a dull, wandering daydream, he felt a movement at his elbow. Looking up, he saw Sosheh, the finisher, furtively reaching for a crust that had dropped from his thick slice of bread.

"You don't want it yet?" she questioned, her face colouring with confusion.

"No," he answered, surprised out of his silence. "But didn't you have any lunch?"

"I'm saving myself from my lunches to buy me a red feather on my new spring hat."

He looked at Sosheh curiously, and noticed for the first time the pinched look of the pale young face.

"Red over that olive paleness!" he mused. "How bright and singing that colour would be!"

Moved by an impulse of friendliness, he pushed an apple towards her.

"Take it," he said. "I had one for my lunch already."

He watched her with smiling interest as she bit hungrily into the juicy fruit.

"Will your feather be as red as this apple?" he asked.

"*Ach!*" she said, with her mouth full. "If you could only give a look how that feather is to me becoming! The redness waves over my black hair like waves from red wine!"

"Why, that girl is a poet!" he thought, thrilled by the way her mind leaped in her dumb yearning for beauty.

The next noon she appeared with a paper bag in her hand. Reverently she drew forth a bright red cock's feather.

"Nu, ain't it grand? For two weeks my lunch money it is."

"How they want to shine, the driven things, even in the shop!" he mused. "Starving for a bit of bright colour—denying themselves food for the shimmering touch of a little beauty!"

One morning, when he had risen to go to work in the grey dawn, he found his landlady bending over an ironing board in the dim gaslight, pressing a child's white dress. She put down the iron to give Berel his breakfast.

"My little Gittel is going to speak a piece to-day." Her face glowed as she showed him the frock. "Give a look only on those flowers I stitched out myself on the sash. Don't they smell almost the fields to you?"

He gazed in wonder at the mother's face beaming down at him. How could Tzipeh Yenteh still sense the perfume of the fields in this dead grind of work? How could his care-crushed landlady, with seven hungry mouths to feed—how could she still reach out for the beautiful? His path to work was lit up by Tzipeh Yenteh's face as she showed him her Gittel's dress in all its freshness.

Little by little he found himself becoming interested in the people about him. Each had his own hidden craving. Each one longed for something beautiful that was his and no one else's.

Beauty—beauty! *Ach*, the lure of it, the tender hope of it! How it filled every heart with its quickening breath! It made no difference what form it took—whether it was the craving for a bright feather, a passion for an ideal, or the love of man for woman. Behind it all was the same flaming hope, the same deathless outreaching for the higher life!

God, what a song to sing! The imperishable glamour of beauty, painting the darkest sweatshop in rainbow colours of heaven, splashing the gloom of the human ant-hill with the golden pigments of sunrise and sunset!

Lifted to winged heights by the onrush of this new vision, Berel swept home with the other toilers pouring from shops and factories.

How thankful he was for the joy of his bleak little room! He shut the door, secure in his solitude. Voices began to speak to him. Faces began to shine for him—the dumb, the oppressed, the toil-driven multitudes who lived and breathed unconscious of the cryings-out in them. All the thwarted longings of their lives, all the baffled feelings of their hearts, all the aching dumbness of their lips, rose to his sympathetic lips, singing the song of the imperishable soul in them.

Berel thought how Beethoven lay prone on the ground, his deaf ears hearing the beat of insects' wings, the rustle of grass, the bloom of buds, all the myriad voices of the pregnant earth. For the first time since the loss of his gift in the jazz pit of Tin Pan Alley, the young poet heard the rhythm of divine creation.

He drew a sheet of white paper before his eyes. From his trembling fingers flowed a poem that wrote its own music—every line a song—the whole a symphony of his regeneration.

"To think that I once despised them—my own people!" he mused. "*Ach*, I was too dense with young pride to see them then!"

His thoughts digging down into the soil of his awakened spirit, he cried aloud:

"Beauty is everywhere, but I can sing it only of my own people. Some one will find it even in Tin Pan Alley—among Maizie's life-loving crowd; but I, in this life, must be the poet of the factories—of my own East Side!"

§ 7

"It's me—Hanneh Breineh!"

A loud thumping at the door and a shrill chatter of voices broke in upon Berel's meditations.

"Me—Moisheh!"

"Come in!" he cried, welcoming this human inbreak after his long vigil.

"Here we got him!" Berel was smothered in Hanneh Breineh's gushing embrace. "Where did you run away that time, you crazy? Don't you yet know my bitter heart? I never mean nothing when I curse."

"For months it dried out our eyes from our heads looking for you," gulped Moisheh, tearing him from Hanneh's greedy arms.

Berel fell on his brother's neck, weeping out the whole rush and tide of his new-born humility.

"Mine own brother, with the old shine from his eyes!"

Moisheh held Berel off, then crushed him in another long hug. Hanneh Breineh, with ostentatious importance, held up her capacious market basket and drew forth a greasy bundle.

"Let's make from it a holiday, for good luck. It's only a bargain, this apple strudel," she said apologetically, breaking it in pieces and giving one to each.

Berel's tears rang out in laughter.

"My own hearts—my own people!"

"*Mazeltuf!* Good luck!" chanted Hanneh Breineh, sipping hungrily the last drops of luscious juice that oozed from the apple strudel.

Raising his piece on high, Moisheh chimed in:

"Good luck and the new life!"

THE LORD GIVETH

One glance at his wife's tight-drawn mouth warned Reb Ravinsky of the torrent of wrath about to burst over his head.

"Nu, my bread-giver? Did you bring me the rent?" she hurled at him between clenched teeth.

Reb Ravinsky had promised to borrow money that morning to ward off their impending eviction for unpaid rent, but no sooner had he stepped out of his house than all thought of it fled from his mind. Instinctively, he turned to the synagogue where he had remained all day absorbed in the sacred script. It was easier to pray and soar the heights with the prophets of his race than to wrestle with sordid, earthly cares.

"Holy Jew! Why didn't you stay away a little longer?" She tore at her wig in her fury. "Are you a man like other men? Does your wife or your child lay in your head at all? I got to worry for rent. I got to worry for bread. If you got to eat you eat. If you ain't got to eat you ain't hungry. You fill yourself only with high thoughts. You hold yourself only with God. Your wife and your child can be thrown in the street to shame and to laughter. But what do you care? You live only for the next world. You got heaven in your head. The rest of your family can rot in the streets."

Reb Ravinsky stood mute and helpless under the lash of her tongue. But when she had exhausted her store of abuse, he cast upon her a look of scorn and condemnation.

"*Ishah Rah!* Evil woman!" he turned upon her like an ancient prophet denouncing ungodliness.

"*Ishah Rah!*" he repeated. His voice of icy passion sent shivers up and down her spine.

"*Ishah Rah!*" came for the third time with the mystic solemnity that subdued her instantly into worshipful subjection. "Tear away your man from God! Tear him away from the holy Torah! Lose the one precious thing in life, the one thing that makes a Jew stand out over all other nations of the world, the one thing that the Tsar's *pogroms* and all the sufferings and murders of the Jews could not kill in the Jew—the hope for the next world!"

Like a towering spirit of righteousness afire with the Word of God he loomed over her.

"I ask you by your conscience, should I give up the real life, the true life, for good eating, good sleeping, for a life in the body like the *Amoratzim* here in

America? Should I make from the Torah a pick with which to dig for you the rent?"

Adjusting his velvet skull-cap, the last relic of his rabbinical days, he caught the woman's adoring look. Memories of his past splendour in Russia surged over him. He saw his people coming to him from far and near to learn wisdom from his lips. Drawing himself to his full height, he strode across the room and faced her.

"Why didn't you marry yourself to a tailor, a shoemaker, a thick-head, a money-maker—to a man of the flesh—a rabbi who can sell his religion over the counter as a butcher sells meat?"

Mrs. Ravinsky gazed with fear and contrition at her husband's God-kindled face. She loved him because he was *not* a man of this world. Her darkest moments were lit up with pride in him, with the hope that in the next world the reflected glory of his piety might exalt her.

It wrung her heart to realize that against her will she was dragging him down with her ceaseless demands for bread and rent. Ach! Why was there such an evil thing as money in this world? Why did she have to torture her husband with earthly needs when all she longed for was to help him win a higher place in heaven?

Tears fell from her faded eyes. He could have wept with her—it hurt him so to make her suffer. But once and for all he must put a stop to her nagging. He must cast out the evil spirit of worry that possessed her lest it turn and rend him.

"Why are you killing yourself so for this life? *Ut!* See, death is already standing over you. One foot is already in the grave. Do you know what you'll get for making nothing from the Torah? The fires of hell are waiting for you! Wait—wait! I warn you!"

And as though to ward off the evil that threatened his house, he rushed to his shrine of sacred books and pulled from its niche a volume of his beloved Talmud. With reverence he caressed its worn and yellowed pages as he drank in hungrily the inspired words. For a few blessed moments he took refuge from all earthly storms.

In Schnipishock, Reb Ravinsky had been a *porush*, a pensioned scholar. The Jews of the village so deeply appreciated his learning and piety that they granted him an allowance, so as to free the man of God from all earthly cares.

Arrived in the new world, he soon learned that there was no honoured pension forthcoming to free him from the world of the flesh. For a time he eked out a bare living by teaching Hebrew to private scholars. But the opening of the Free Hebrew Schools resulted in the loss of most of his pupils.

He had been chosen by God to spread the light of the Torah—and a living must come to him, somehow, somewhere, if he only served faithfully.

In the meantime, how glorious it was to suffer hunger and want, even shame and derision, yet rise through it all as Job had risen and proclaim to the world: "I know that my Redeemer liveth!"

Reb Ravinsky was roused from his ecstasy by his wife's loud sobbing. Thrust out from the haven of his Torah, he closed the book and began to pace the floor.

"Can fire and water go together? Neither can godliness and an easy life. If you have eyes of flesh and are blind, should I fall into your blindness? You care only for what you can put in your mouth or wear on your back; I struggle for the life that is together with God!"

"My rent—have you my rent? I warned you!" The landlord pushed through the half-open door flaunting his final dispossess notice under Reb Ravinsky's nose. "I got orders to put you out," he gloated, as he motioned to his men to proceed with the eviction.

Reb Ravinsky gripped the back of a chair for support.

"Oi-i-i! Black is me! Bitter is me!" groaned his wife, leaning limply against the wall.

For weeks she had been living in momentary dread of this catastrophe. Now, when the burly moving men actually broke into her home, she surrendered herself to the anguish of utter defeat. She watched them disconnect the rusty stove and carry it into the street. They took the bed, the Passover dishes prayerfully wrapped to avoid the soil of leavened bread. They took the brass samovar and the Sabbath candlesticks. And she stood mutely by—defenceless—impotent!

"What did I sin?" The cry broke from her. "God! God! Is there a God over us and sees all this?"

The men and the things they touched were to Reb Ravinsky's far-seeing eyes as shadows of the substanceless dream of life in the flesh. With vision focused on the next world, he saw in dim blurs the drama enacted in this world.

Smash to the floor went the sacred Sabbath wineglass! Reb Ravinsky turned sharply, in time to see a man tumble ruthlessly the sacred Hebrew books to the floor.

A flame of holy wrath leaped from the old man's eyes. His breath came in convulsive gasps as he clutched with emaciated fingers at his heart. The sacrilege of the ruffians! He rushed to pick up the books, kissing each volume with pious reverence. As he gathered them in his trembling arms, he looked about confusedly for a safe hiding-place. In his anxiety for the safety of his holy treasure, he forgot the existence of his wife and ran with his books to the synagogue as one runs from a house on fire. So overwrought was he that he nearly fell over his little daughter running up the stairs.

"Murderer!" screamed Mrs. Ravinsky, after him. "Run, run to the synagogue! Holy Jew! See where your religion has brought us. Run—ask God to pay your rent!"

She turned to her little Rachel who burst into the room terrified.

"See, my heart! See what they've done to us! And your father ran to hide himself in the synagogue. You got no father—nobody to give you bread. A lost orphan you are."

"Will the charity lady have to bring us eating again?" asked Rachel, her eyes dilated with dread. "Wait only till I get old enough to go to the shop and earn money." And she reached up little helpless arms protectingly.

The child's sympathy was as salt on the mother's wounds.

"For what did we come to America?"

The four walls of her broken home stared back their answer.

Only the bundles of bedding remained, which Rachel guarded with fierce defiance as though she would save it from the wreckage.

Pushing the child roughly aside, the man slung it over his shoulder. Mrs. Ravinsky, with Rachel holding on to her skirts, felt her way after him down the dark stairway.

"My life! My blood! My feather bed!" she cried, as he tossed the family heirloom into the gutter. "Gevalt!" prostrate, she fell on it. "How many winters it took my mother to pick together the feathers! My mother's wedding present...."

From the stoops, the alleys and the doorways the neighbours gathered. Hanneh Breineh, followed by her clinging brood, pushed through the throng, her red-lidded eyes big with compassion. "Come the while in by me."

She helped the grief-stricken woman to her feet. "We're packed like herrings in a barrel, but there's always room for a push-in of a few more."

Lifting the feather bed under her arm she led the way to her house.

"In a few more years your Rachel will be old enough to get her working papers and all your worries for bread will be over," she encouraged, as she opened the door of her stuffy little rooms.

The commotion on the street corner broke in upon the babble of gossiping women in the butcher shop. Mr. Sopkin paused in cutting the meat.

"Who did they make to move?" he asked, joining the gesticulating mob at the doorway.

"*Oi weh!* Reb Ravinsky?"

"God from the sky! Such a good Jew! Such a light for the world!"

"Home, in Russia, they kissed the ground on which he walked, and in America they throw him in the street!"

"Who cares in America for religion? In America everybody has his head in his belly."

"Poor little Rachel! Such a smart child! Writes letters for everybody on the block."

"Such a lazy do-nothing! All day in the synagogue!" flung the pawnbroker's wife, a big-bosomed woman, her thick fingers covered with diamonds. "Why don't he go to work in a shop?"

A neighbour turned upon her. "Hear! Hear her only! Such a pig-eater! Such a fat-head! She dares take Reb Ravinsky's name in her mouth."

"Who was she from home? A water-carrier's wife, a cook! And in America she makes herself for a person—shines up the street with her diamonds."

"Then leave somebody let know the charities." With a gesture of self-defence, the pawnbroker's wife fingered her gold beads. "I'm a lady-member from the charities."

"The charities? A black year on them!" came a chorus of angry voices.

"All my enemies should have to go to the charities for help."

"Woe to anyone who falls into the charities' hands!"

"One poor man with a heart can help more than the charities with all their money."

Mr. Sopkin hammered on his chopping-block, his face purple with excitement. "*Weiber!* with talk alone you can't fill up the pot."

"*Takeh! Takeh!*" Eager faces strained forward. "Let's put ourselves together for a collection."

"I'm not yet making Rockefeller's millions from the butcher business, but still, here's my beginning for good luck." And Mr. Sopkin tossed a dollar bill into the basket on the counter.

A woman, a ragged shawl over her head, clutched a quarter in her gaunt hand. "God is my witness! To tear out this from my pocket is like tearing off my right hand. I need every cent to keep the breath in the bodies of my *kinder*, but how can we let such a holy Jew fall in the street?"

"My enemies should have to slave with such bitter sweat for every penny as me." Hannah Hayyeh flung out her arms still wet with soapsuds and kissed the ten-cent piece she dropped into the collection.

Mr. Sopkin walked to the sidewalk and shook the basket in front of the passers-by. "Take your hand out from your pocket! Take your bite away from your mouth! Who will help the poor if not the poor?"

A shower of coins came pouring in. It seemed not money—but the flesh and blood of the people—each coin a part of a living heart.

The pawnbroker's wife, shamed by the surging generosity of the crowd, grudgingly peeled a dollar from the roll of bills in her stocking and started to put it into the collection.

A dozen hands lifted in protest.

"No—no! Your money and our money can't mix together!"

"Our money is us—our bodies! Yours is the profits from the pawnshop! Hold your *trefah* dollar for the charities!"

Only when the Shammes, the caretaker of the synagogue, rattling his keys, shook Reb Ravinsky gently and reminded him that it was past closing time did he remember that somewhere waiting for him—perhaps still in the street—were his wife and child.

The happening of the day had only deepened the intensity with which he clung to God and His Torah. His lips still moved in habitual prayer as with the guidance of neighbours he sought the new flat which had been rented for a month with the collection money.

Bread, butter, milk and eggs greeted his gaze as he opened the door.

"*Nu*, my wife? Is there a God over us?" His face kindled with guileless faith. "The God that feeds the little fishes in the sea and the birds in the air, has He not fed us? You see, the Highest One takes care of our earthly needs. Our only business here is to pray for holiness to see His light!"

A cloud of gloom stared up at him out of his wife's darkening eyes.

"Why are you still so black with worry?" he admonished. "If you would only trust yourself on God, all good would come to us yet."

"On my enemies should fall the good that has come to us," groaned Mrs. Ravinsky. "Better already death than to be helped again by the pity from kind people."

"What difference how the help comes, so long we can keep up our souls to praise God for His mercy on us?"

Despair was in the look she fixed upon her husband's lofty brow—a brow untouched by time or care, smooth, calm and seamless as a child's. "No wonder people think that I'm your mother. The years make you younger. You got no blood in your body—no feelings in your heart. I got to close my eyes with shame to pass in the street the people what helped me, while you— you—shame cannot shame you—poverty cannot crush you———"

"Poverty? It stands in the Talmud that poverty is an ornament on a Jew like a red ribbon on a white horse. Those whom God chooses for His next world can't have it good here."

"Stop feeding me with the next world!" she flung at him in her exasperation. "Give me something on this world."

"Wait only till our American daughter will grow up. That child has my head on her," he boasted with a father's pride. "Wait only, you'll see the world will ring from her yet. With the Hebrew learning I gave her, she'll shine out from all other American children."

"But how will she be able to lift up her head with other people alike if you depend yourself on the charities?"

"Woman! Worry yourself not for our Rachel! It stands in the Holy Book, the world is a wheel, always turning. Those who are rich get poor; if not they, then their children or children's children. And those who are poor like us, go up higher and higher. Our daughter will yet be so rich, she'll give away money to the charities that helped us. Isaiah said———"

"Enough—enough!" broke in Mrs. Ravinsky, thrilled in spite of herself by the prophecies of her holy man. "I know already all your smartness. Go, go, sit yourself down and eat something. You fasted all day."

Mrs. Ravinsky hoarded for her husband and child the groceries the neighbours had donated. For herself she allowed only the left-overs, the crumbs and crusts.

The following noon, after finishing her meagre meal, she still felt the habitual gnawing of her under-nourished body, so she took a sour pickle and cut off another slice of bread from the dwindling loaf. But this morsel only sharpened her craving for more food.

The lingering savour of the butter and eggs which she had saved for her family tantalized her starved nerves. Faint and weak from the struggle to repress her hunger, she grew reckless and for once in her life abandoned herself to the gluttonous indulgence of the best in her scant larder.

With shaking hand she stealthily opened the cupboard, pilfered a knife-load of butter and spread it thickly on a second slice of bread. Cramming the whole into her mouth, she snatched two eggs and broke them into the frying-pan. The smell of the sizzling eggs filled the air with the sweet fragrance of the Sabbath. "Ach! How the sun would shine in my heart if I could only allow myself the bite in my mouth!"

Memories of *gefüllte* fish and the odour of freshly-baked apple strudel dilated her nostrils. She saw herself back in Russia setting the Sabbath table when she was the honoured wife of Reb Ravinsky.

The sudden holiday feeling that thrilled her senses smote her conscience. "Oi weh! Sinner that I am! Why should it will itself in me to eat like a person when my man don't earn enough for dry bread? What will we do when this is used up? Suppose the charities should catch me feasting myself with such a full hand?"

Bent ravenously over the eggs—one eye on the door—she lifted the first spoonful to her watering mouth as Rachel flew in, eyes wide with excitement.

"Mamma! The charity lady is coming! She's asking the fish-pedlar on the stoop where we live now."

"Quick! Hide the frying-pan in the oven! Woe is me! The house not swept—dishes not washed—everything thrown around! Rachel! Quick only—sweep together the dirt in a corner. Throw those rags under the bed! *Oi weh*—quick—hide all those dirty things behind the trunk!"

In her haste to tidy up, she remembered the food in the cupboard. She stuffed it—broken eggshells and all—into the bureau drawer. "Oi weh! The charity lady should only not catch us with all these holiday eatings...."

Footsteps in the hallway and Miss Naughton's cheery voice: "Here I am, Mrs. Ravinsky! What can I do to help now?"

With the trained eye of the investigator, she took in the wretched furniture, scant bedding, the under-nourished mother and child.

"What seems to be wrong?" Miss Naughton drew up a three-legged stool. "Won't you tell me, so we can get at the root of the trouble?" She put her hand on the woman's apron with a friendly little gesture.

Mrs. Ravinsky bit her lips to force back the choking pressure of tears. The life, the buoyancy, the very kindness of the "charity lady" stabbed deeper the barb of her wretchedness.

"Woe is me! On all my enemies my black heart! So many babies and young people die every day, but no death comes to hide me from my shame."

"Don't give way like that," pleaded Miss Naughton, pained by the bitterness that she tried in vain to understand. "If you will only tell me a few things so I may the better know how to help you."

"Again tear me in pieces with questions?" Mrs. Ravinsky pulled at the shrunken skin of her neck.

"I don't like to pry into your personal affairs, but if you only knew how often we're imposed upon. Last week we had a case of a woman who asked us to pay her rent. When I called to investigate, I found her cooking chicken for dinner!"

The cot on which Mrs. Ravinsky sat creaked under her swaying body.

"You see, we have only a small amount of money," went on the unconscious inquisitor, "and it is but fair it should go to the most deserving cases."

Entering a few preliminary notes, Miss Naughton looked up inquiringly. "Where is Mr. Ravinsky?"

"In the synagogue."

"Has he no work?"

"He can't do no work. His head is on the next world."

Miss Naughton frowned. She was accustomed to this kind of excuse. "People who are not lazy can always find employment."

Seeing Mrs. Ravinsky's sudden pallor, she added kindly: "You have not eaten to-day. Is there no food in the house?"

Mrs. Ravinsky staggered blindly to her feet. "No—nothing—I didn't yet eat nothing."

The brooding grey of Rachel's eyes darkened with shame as she clutched protectingly at her mother's apron. The uncanny, old look of the solemn little face seemed to brush against Miss Naughton's very heartstrings—to reproach the rich vigour of her own glowing youth.

"Have you had any lunch, dear?" The "charity lady's" hand rested softly on the tangled mat of hair.

"N-nothing—nothing," the child echoed her mother's words.

Miss Naughton rose abruptly. She dared not let her feelings get the better of her. "I am going to get some groceries." She sought for an excuse to get away for a moment from the misery that overwhelmed her. "I'll be back soon."

"Bitter is me!" wailed Mrs. Ravinsky, as the "charity lady" left the room. "I can never lift up my head with other people alike. I feel myself lower than a thief, just because I got a husband who holds himself with God all day."

She cracked the knuckles of her bony fingers. "*Gottuniu!* Listen better to my prayer! Send on him only a quick death. Maybe if I was a widow, people would take pity on me and save me from this gehenna of charity."

Ten minutes later Miss Naughton returned with a bag of supplies. "I am going to fix some lunch for you." She measured cocoa into a battered saucepan. "And soon the boy will come with enough groceries for the whole week."

"Please, please," begged Mrs. Ravinsky. "I can't eat now—I can't."

"But the child? She needs nutritious food at once."

Rachel's sunken little chest rose and fell with her frightened heartbeat as she hid her face in her mother's lap.

"Small as she is, she already feels how it hurts to swallow charity eating," defended Mrs. Ravinsky.

Miss Naughton could understand the woman's dislike of accepting charity. She had coped with this pride of the poor before. But she had no sympathy with this mother who fostered resentment in her child towards the help that was so urgently needed. Miss Naughton's long-suffering patience broke. She turned from the stove and resolutely continued her questioning.

"Has your husband tried our employment bureau?"

"No."

"Then send him to our office to-morrow at nine. He can be a janitor—or a porter——"

"My man? My man a janitor or a porter?" Her eyes flamed. "Do you know who was my man in Russia? The fat of the land they brought him just for the pleasure to listen to his learning. Barrels full of meat, pots full of chicken fat stood packed in my cellar. I used to make boilers of jelly at a time. The *gefüllte* fish only I gave away is more than the charities give out to the poor in a month."

Miss Naughton could not suppress a smile. "Why did you leave it, then, if it was all so perfect?"

"My *gefüllte* fish! Oi-i-i! Oi-i!! My apple strudel!" she kept repeating, unable to tear herself away from the dream of the past.

"Can you live on the apple strudel you had in Russia? In America a man must work to support his family——"

"All thick-heads support their families," defended Reb Ravinsky's wife. "Any fat-belly can make money. My man is a light for the world. He works for God who feeds even the worms under the stone."

"You send your husband to my office. I want to have a talk with him."

"To your office? *Gottuniu!* He won't go. In Schnipishock they came to him from the four ends of the world. The whole town blessed itself with his religiousness."

"The first principle of religion is for a man to provide for his family. You must do exactly as we say—or we cannot help you."

"Please, please!" Mrs. Ravinsky entreated, cringing and begging. "We got no help from nobody now but you. I'll bring him to your office to-morrow."

The investigator now proceeded with the irk-some duty of her more formal questions. "How much rent do you pay? Do you keep any boarders? Does your husband belong to any society or lodge? Have you relatives who are able to help you?"

"Oi-i-i! What more do you want from me?" shrieked the distracted woman.

Having completed her questions, Miss Naughton looked about the room. "I am sorry to speak of it, but why is your flat in such disorder?"

"I only moved in yesterday. I didn't get yet time to fix it up."

"But it was just as bad in the last place. If you want our help you must do your part. Soap and water are cheap. Anyone can be clean."

The woman's knees gave way under her, as Miss Naughton lifted the lids from the pots on the stove.

And then—*gevalt*! It grew black before Mrs. Ravinsky's eyes. She collapsed into a pathetic heap to the floor. The "charity lady" opened the oven door and exposed the tell-tale frying-pan and the two eggs!

Eyes of silent condemnation scorched through the terror-stricken creature whose teeth chattered in a vain struggle to defend herself. But no voice came from her tortured throat. She could only clutch at her child in a panic of helplessness.

Without a word, the investigator began to search through every nook and corner and at last she came to the bureau drawer and found butter, eggs, cheese, bread and even a jar of jelly.

"For shame!" broke from the wounded heart of the betrayed Miss Naughton. "You—you ask for charity!"

In the hall below Reb Ravinsky, returning from the synagogue, encountered a delivery boy.

"Where live the Ravinskys?" the lad questioned.

"I'm Reb Ravinsky," he said, leading the way, as he saw the box of groceries.

Followed by the boy, Reb Ravinsky flung open the door and strode joyfully into the room. "Look only! How the manna is falling from the sky!"

Ignoring Reb Ravinsky, Miss Naughton motioned to the box. "Take those things right back," she commanded the boy.

"How you took me in with your hungry look!" There was more of sorrow than scorn in her voice. "Even teaching your child to lie—and your husband a rabbi!—a religious man—too holy to work! What would be left for deserving cases if we allowed such as you to defraud legitimate charity?"

With bowed head, Reb Ravinsky closed the door after the departing visitor. The upbraidings of the woman were like a whip-lash on his naked flesh. His heart ached for his helpless family. Darkness suffocated him.

"My hungry little lamb," wailed his wife, clinging to Rachel. "Where now can we turn for bread?"

Compassionate hands reached out in prayer over the grief-stricken mother and child. Reb Ravinsky stood again as he did before his flight to America, facing his sorrowing people. His wife's wailing for their lost store of bread brought back to him the bereaved survivors of the *pogrom*—the *pogrom* that snatched away their sons and daughters. Afire with the faith of his race, he chanted the age-old consolation: "The Lord giveth; the Lord taketh away. Blessed be the name of the Lord."

9 789367 241066